ARCTURUS

This edition published in 2024 by Arcturus Publishing Limited
26/27 Bickels Yard, 151–153 Bermondsey Street,
London SE1 3HA

Author: Lisa Regan
Illustrator: Ana Sebastián
Editor: Violet Peto
Designer: Stefan Holliland
Design Manager: Rosie Bellwood-Moyler
Editorial Manager: Joe Harris

ISBN: 978-1-3988-4363-9
CH011567NT
Supplier 29, Date 0824, PI00006227

Printed in China

HOW TO USE THIS BOOK

Welcome to the "funtastic" world of times tables mazes! This activity book is full of exciting scenes to help you learn and become confident with the basics of multiplication and division.

Read the instructions to help you solve the maze.

Some topics come with a **TOP TIP** to help you on the way.

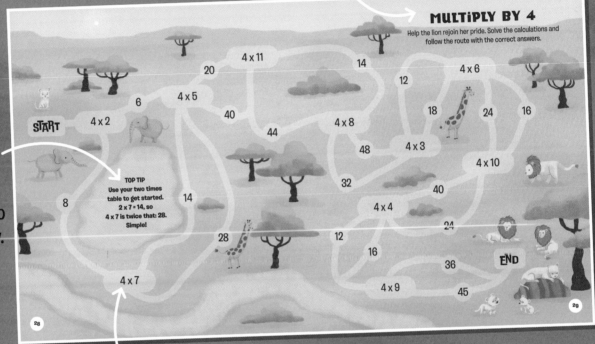

MULTIPLY BY 4

Help the lion rejoin her pride. Solve the calculations and follow the route with the correct answers.

START

4 x 11
4 x 5
4 x 2
4 x 6
4 x 8
4 x 3
4 x 10
4 x 4
4 x 7
4 x 9

TOP TIP
Use your two times table to get started.
2 x 7 = 14, so 4 x 7 is twice that: 28.
Simple!

END

Solve each equation, and then choose the correct path to reach the end.

You can find a times table square to help you on page 96.

After you have completed the maze, check that you followed the correct route by turning to pages 89-96.

DOUBLiNG

Find your way through the fruit market, following the path that uses doubles.

START

3 + 3

2 + 3

6 + 6

4 + 4

5 + 9

8 + 6

7 + 3

5 + 5

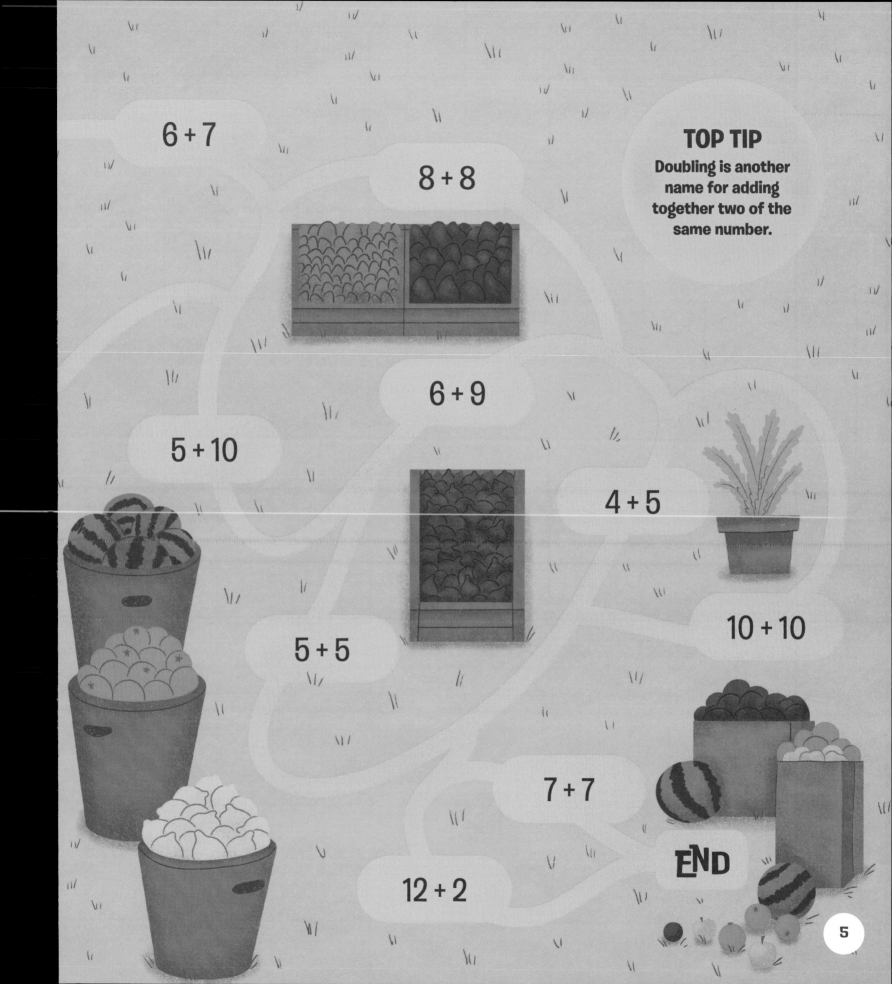

MULTIPLY BY 2

Find a path back to the safari lodge. Work out the calculations and follow the correct answers.

6

5

2 x 3

16

9

START

2 x 7

20

2 x 5

8

2 x 10

14

10

TOP TIP
Multiplying by 2 is the same as doubling a number.

2 x 6

12

14

10

2 x 8

END

8

2 x 4

16

19

2 x 9

18

18

START

3

15

18

4

21

8

20

12

MULTIPLES OF 2

Help the skater link up with his partner by following the multiples of 2.

7

6

10

16

14

END

TOP TIP

Can you count in
twos? Then you
already know
multiples of 2!

9

11

13

5

2

9

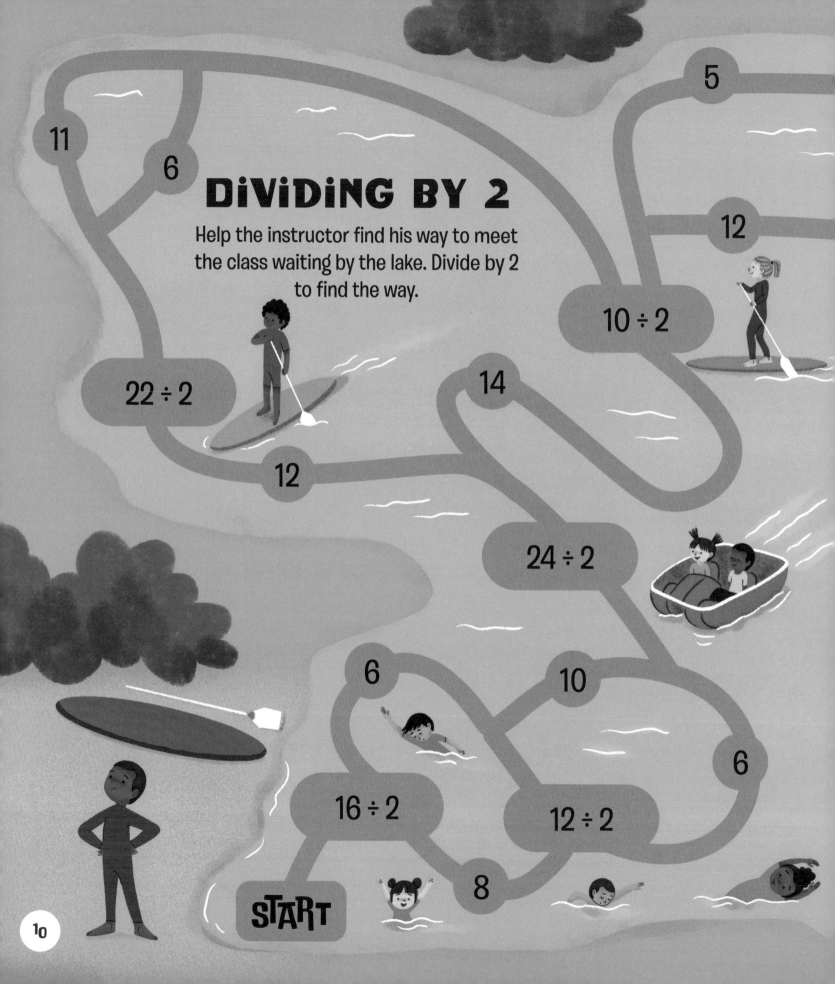

DIVIDING BY 2

Help the instructor find his way to meet the class waiting by the lake. Divide by 2 to find the way.

5

11

6

12

$22 \div 2$

$10 \div 2$

14

12

$24 \div 2$

6

10

6

$16 \div 2$

$12 \div 2$

8

START

MULTIPLY BY 10

Help the mother crocodile reach her babies by using your ten times table.

40

10 x 7

20

START

17

10 x 4

70

10 x 10

44

100

10

TOP TIP
All the answers in
the ten times table
end in a 0.

10 x 8

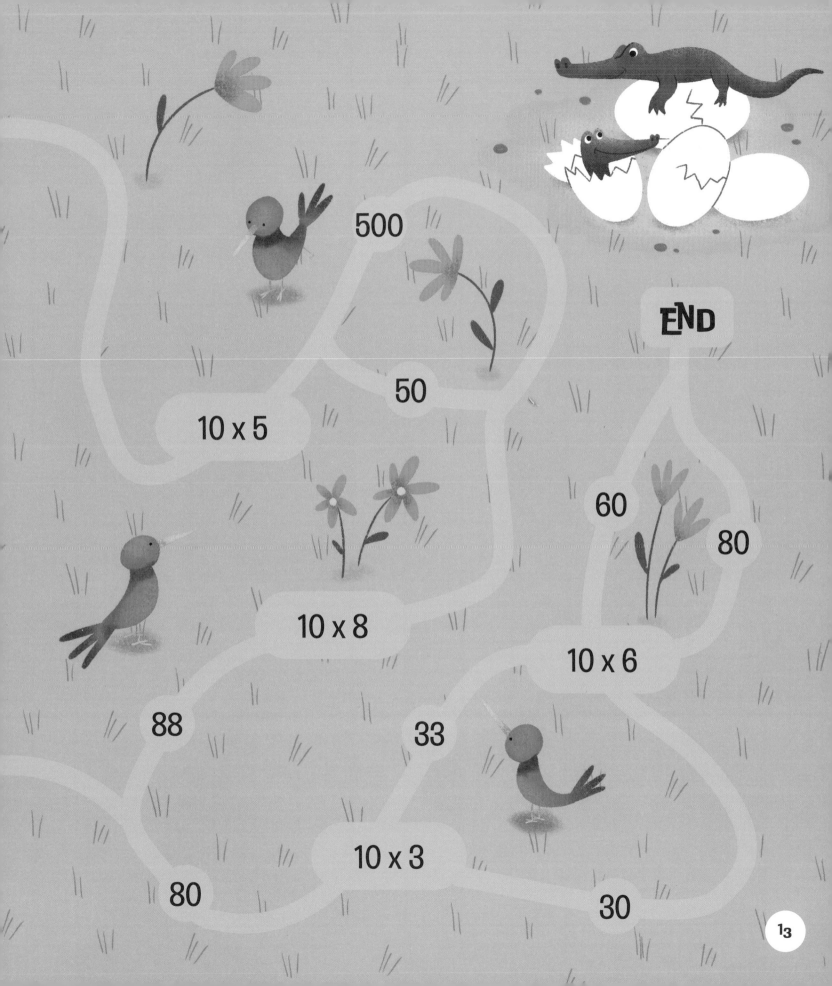

500

END

50

10 x 5

60

80

10 x 8

10 x 6

88

33

10 x 3

80

30

13

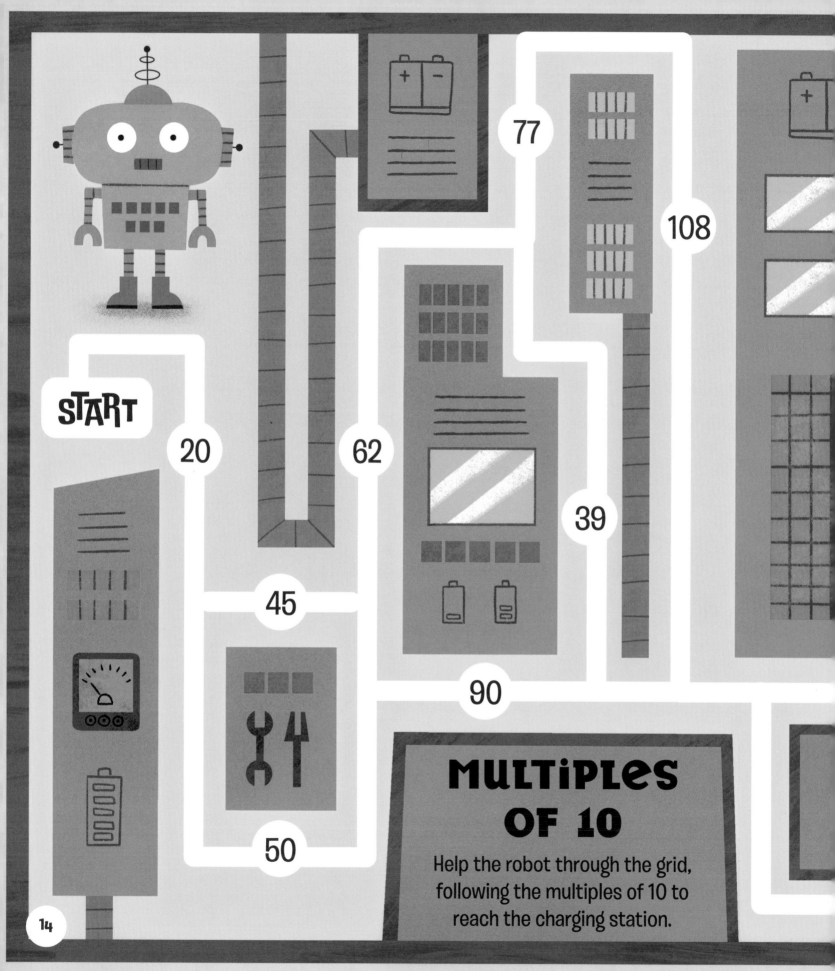

START

20

77

108

62

39

45

90

50

MULTIPLES OF 10

Help the robot through the grid, following the multiples of 10 to reach the charging station.

14

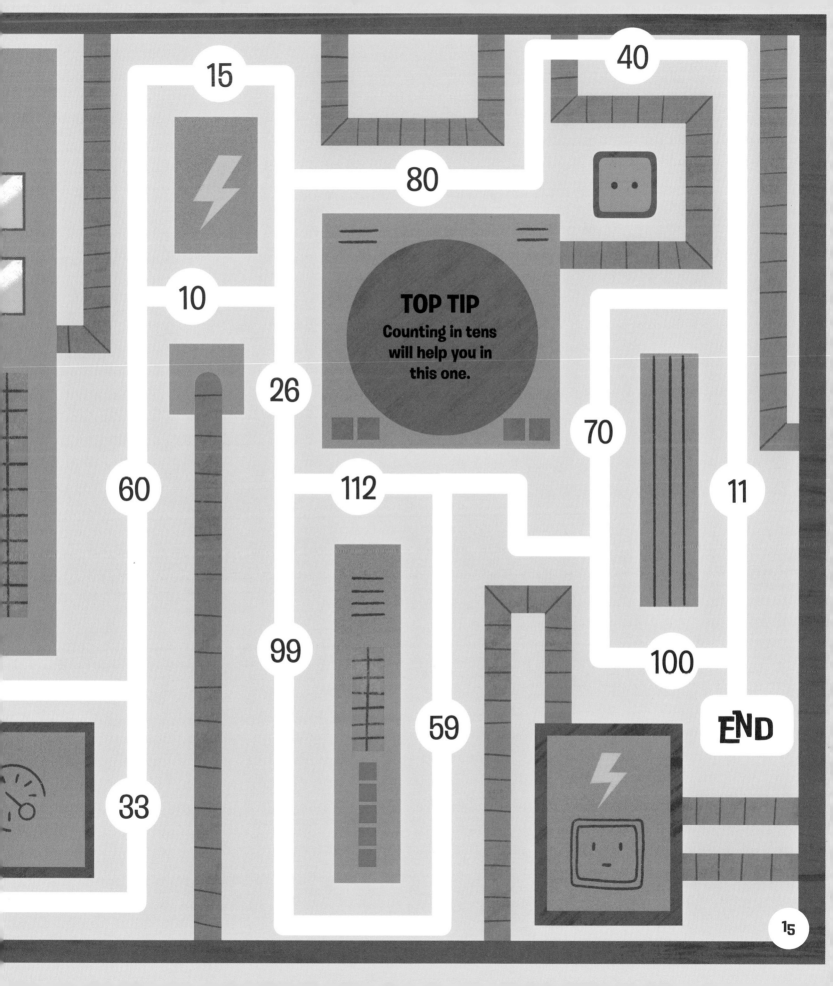

TOP TIP
Counting in tens
will help you in
this one.

END

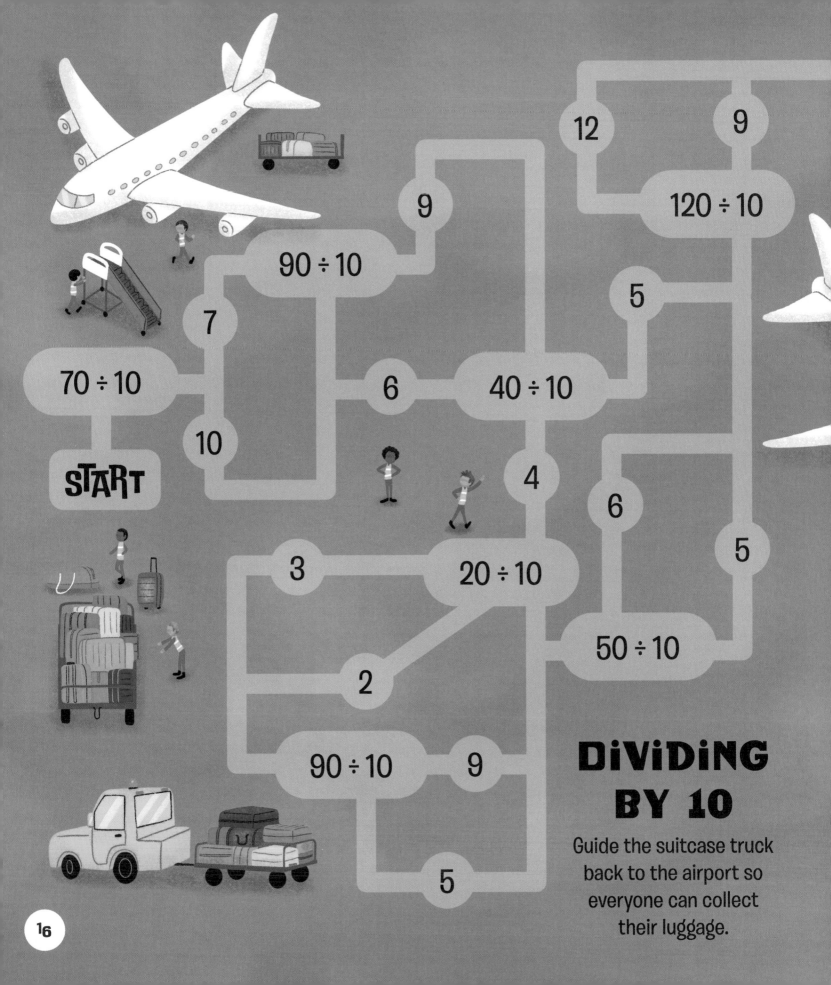

DIVIDING BY 10

Guide the suitcase truck back to the airport so everyone can collect their luggage.

START

70 ÷ 10
7
10
90 ÷ 10
9
12
9
120 ÷ 10
5
6
40 ÷ 10
4
6
5
3
20 ÷ 10
2
50 ÷ 10
90 ÷ 10
9
5

16

30 ÷ 10

3

5

8

80 ÷ 10

18   110 ÷ 10

11

100

TOP TIP
Dividing a number is the same as sharing it. Dividing by 10 is like sharing among ten friends.

60 ÷ 10

END

80

10

6   8

100 ÷ 10

10 ÷ 10   1

20

MULTIPLY BY 5

This mermaid needs to get to singing class.
Guide her there using multiples of five.

18

56

5 x 3

5 x 7

15

35

5 x 5

50

5 x 10

START

55

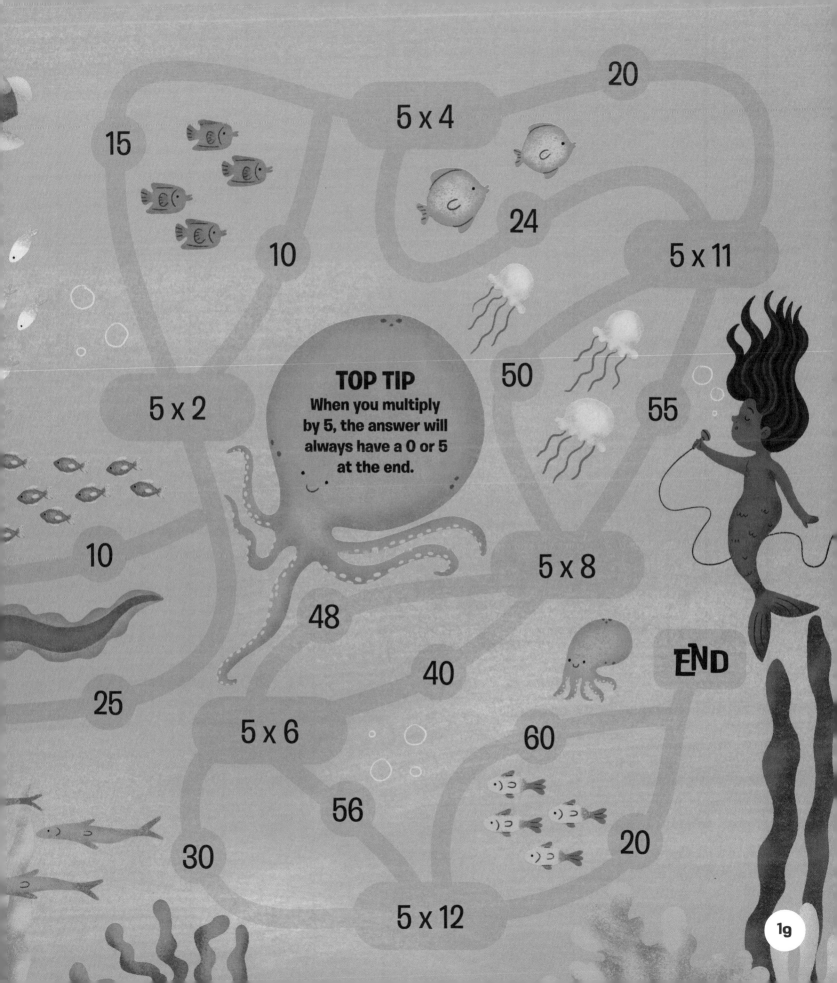

20

5 x 4

15

10

24

5 x 11

TOP TIP
When you multiply
by 5, the answer will
always have a 0 or 5
at the end.

50

55

5 x 2

10

5 x 8

48

END

25

40

5 x 6

60

56

30

20

5 x 12

MULTIPLES OF 5

Help Puss in Boots make his way
to the castle by following numbers
that are multiples of five.

START

18

51

15

TOP TIP
Counting in fives is
a great way to learn
your five times
table.

20

45

35

29

60

DIVIDING BY 5

These monsters are all over the place! Round them up, following the correct answers if you divide by 5.

5

50 ÷ 5

8

11

6

2

10

15 ÷ 5

25 ÷ 5

START

30 ÷ 5

11

8

10 ÷ 5

8

END

20

5

2

12

55 ÷ 5

60 ÷ 5

11

6

40 ÷ 5

9

45 ÷ 5

7

3

TOP TIP

The symbol for dividing is ÷ but you may see it written as /. 25 / 5 is the same as 25 ÷ 5.

35 ÷ 5

6

4

23

MULTIPLES OF 2, 10, AND 5

Solve the problems and help the rocket navigate around the planets and back to Earth.

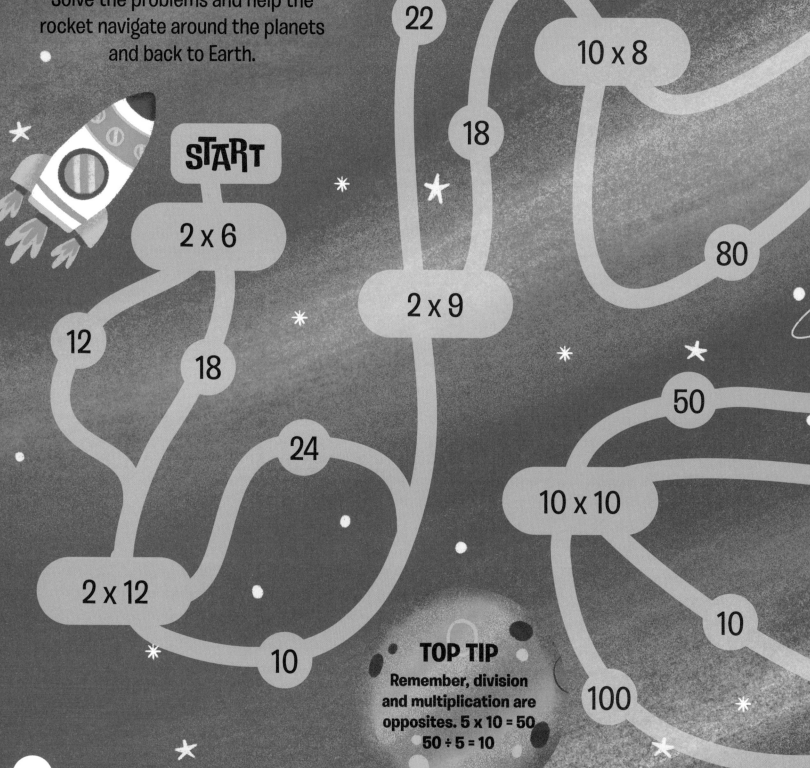

22

10 x 8

18

START

2 x 6

80

2 x 9

12

18

50

24

10 x 10

2 x 12

10

10

100

TOP TIP
Remember, division and multiplication are opposites. 5 x 10 = 50
50 ÷ 5 = 10

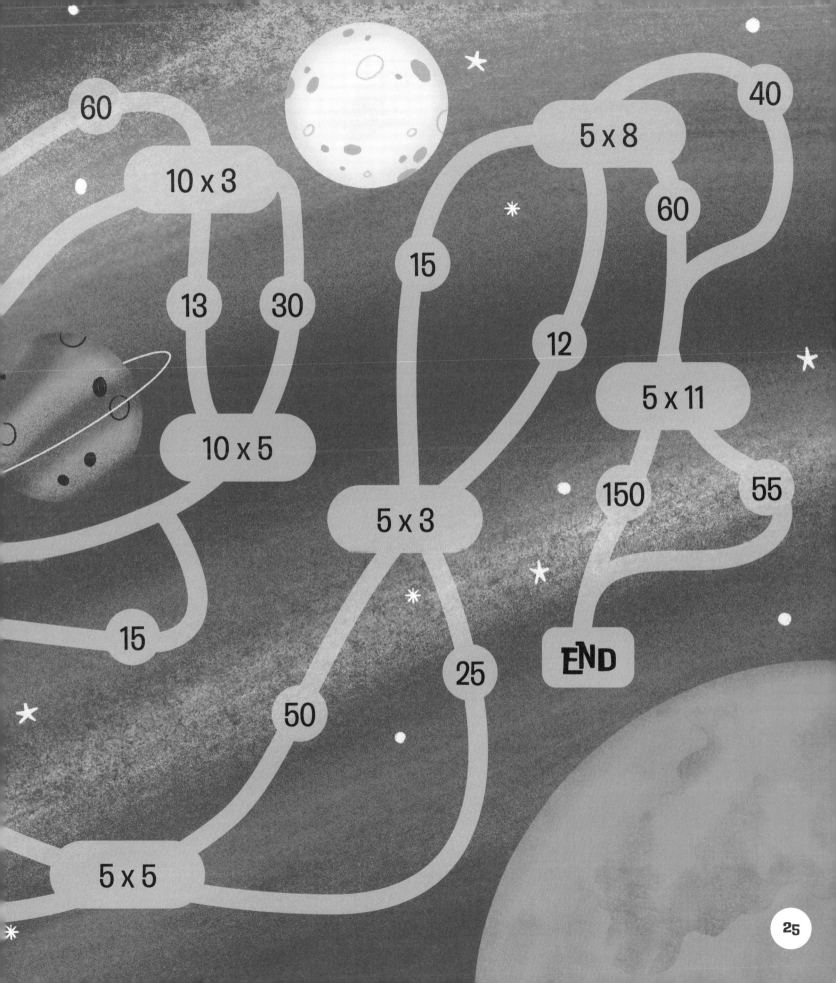

DIVISION OF 2, 10, AND 5

Find the correct answers to help the caterpillar munch his way through the maze.

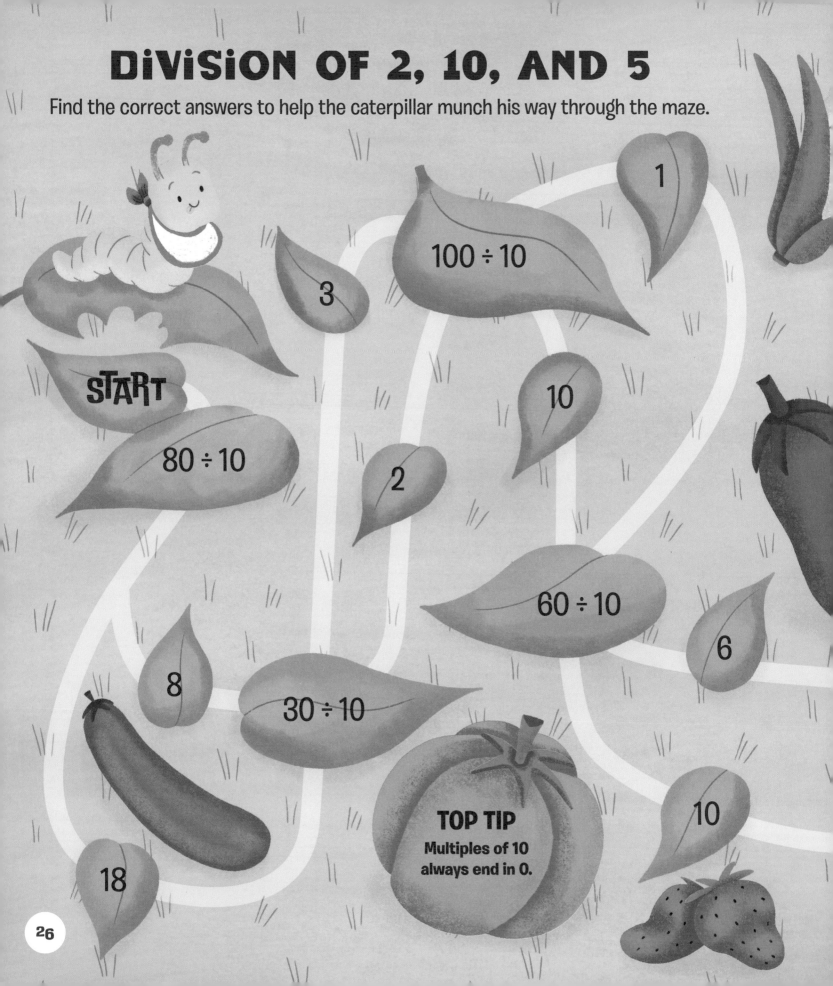

1

$100 \div 10$

3

10

$80 \div 10$

START

2

$60 \div 10$

6

8

$30 \div 10$

TOP TIP
Multiples of 10
always end in 0.

10

18

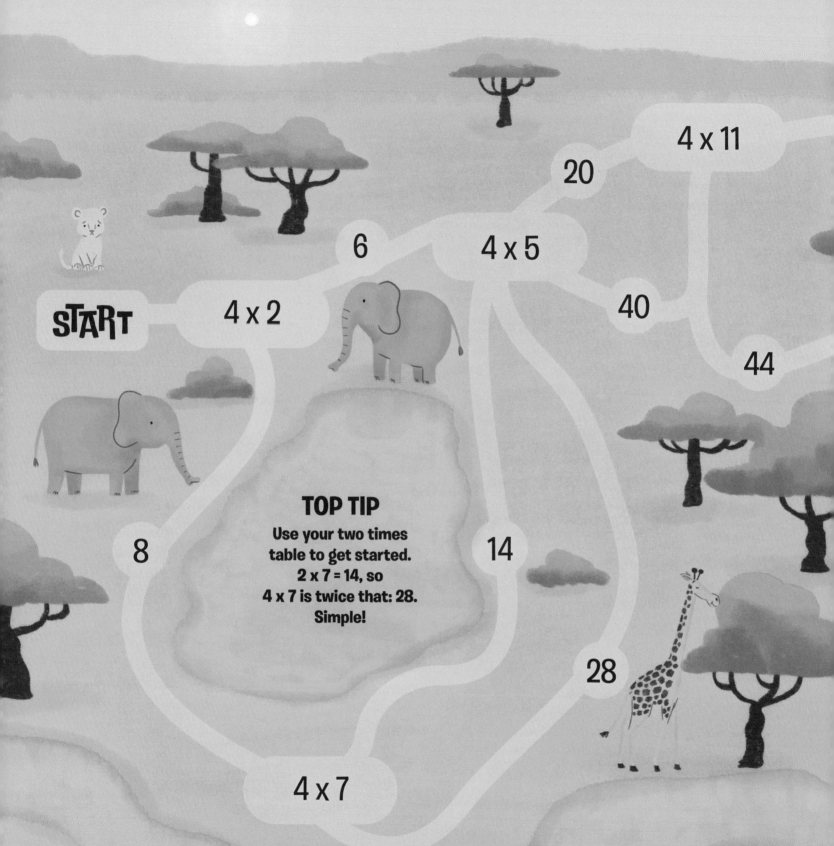

4 x 11

20

6

4 x 5

40

44

START

4 x 2

8

TOP TIP
Use your two times
table to get started.
2 x 7 = 14, so
4 x 7 is twice that: 28.
Simple!

14

28

4 x 7

MULTIPLY BY 4

Help the lion cub rejoin her pride. Solve the calculations
and follow the route with the correct answers.

14

12

4 x 6

4 x 8

18

24

16

48

4 x 3

4 x 10

32

40

4 x 4

24

12

16

END

36

4 x 9

45

MULTiPLES OF 4

The drummer has fallen behind. Help her catch up and follow the correct route, using numbers from the four times table.

48
46
32
34
18
8
20
40
12
44

START

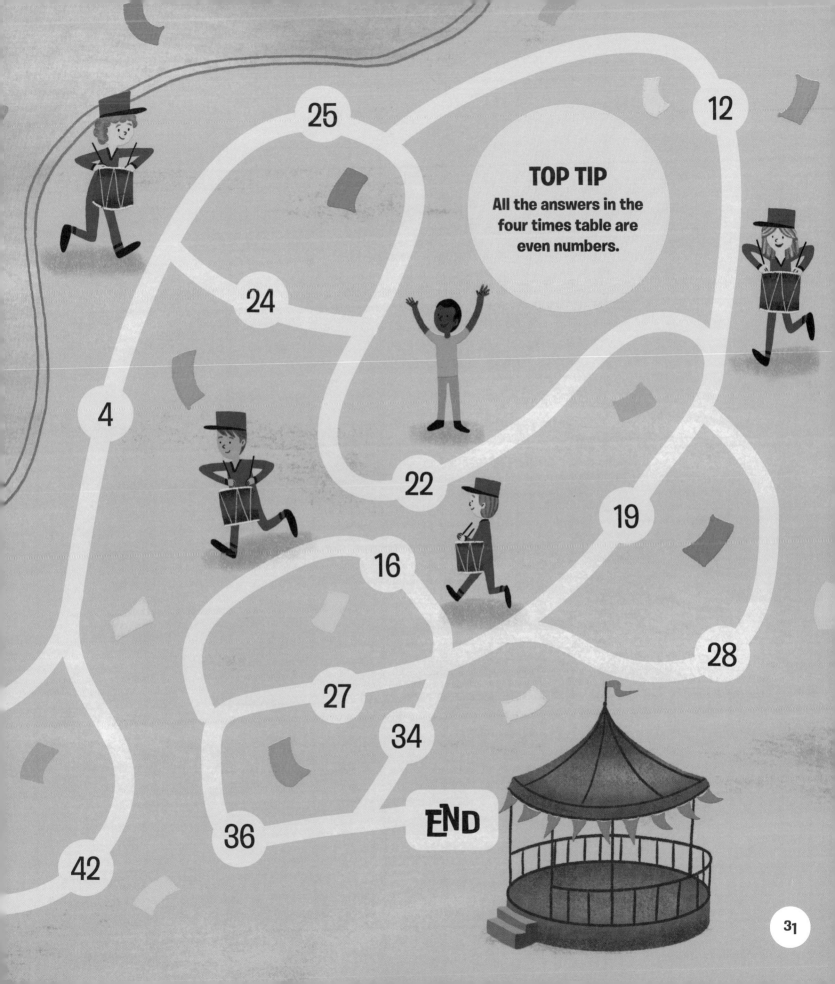

25

12

TOP TIP
All the answers in the
four times table are
even numbers.

24

4

22

19

16

28

27

34

END

36

42

31

48 ÷ 4   9

4

START

16 ÷ 4

12

12 ÷ 4

5

3

4

6

24 ÷ 4

DiViDiNG BY 4

Guide the helicopter through the clouds, dividing by four to find the correct route.

11

32

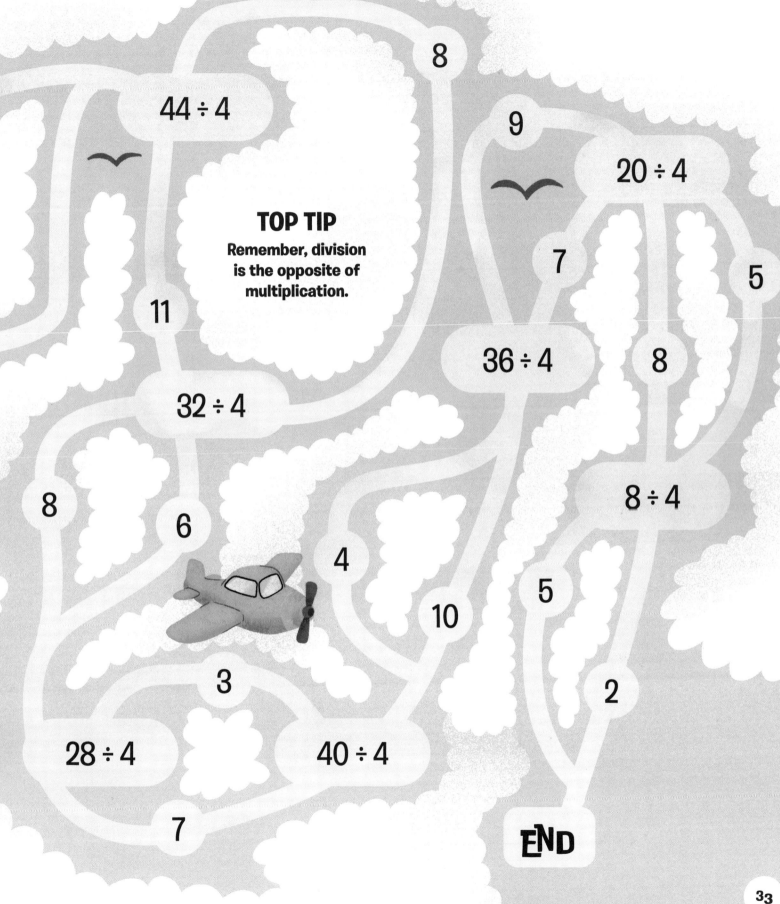

8

44 ÷ 4

9

20 ÷ 4

TOP TIP
Remember, division is the opposite of multiplication.

7

5

11

36 ÷ 4

8

32 ÷ 4

8 ÷ 4

8

6

4

5

10

3

2

28 ÷ 4

40 ÷ 4

7

END

MULTIPLY BY 8

Work out the answers using the eight times table to find a way from start to finish.

TOP TIP
Multiplying is a fast way of adding up.
8 + 8 + 8 + 8 + 8 + 8 is 6 lots of 8.

32

16

68

8 x 4

8 x 10

8 x 8

40

8 x 5

80

60

64

START

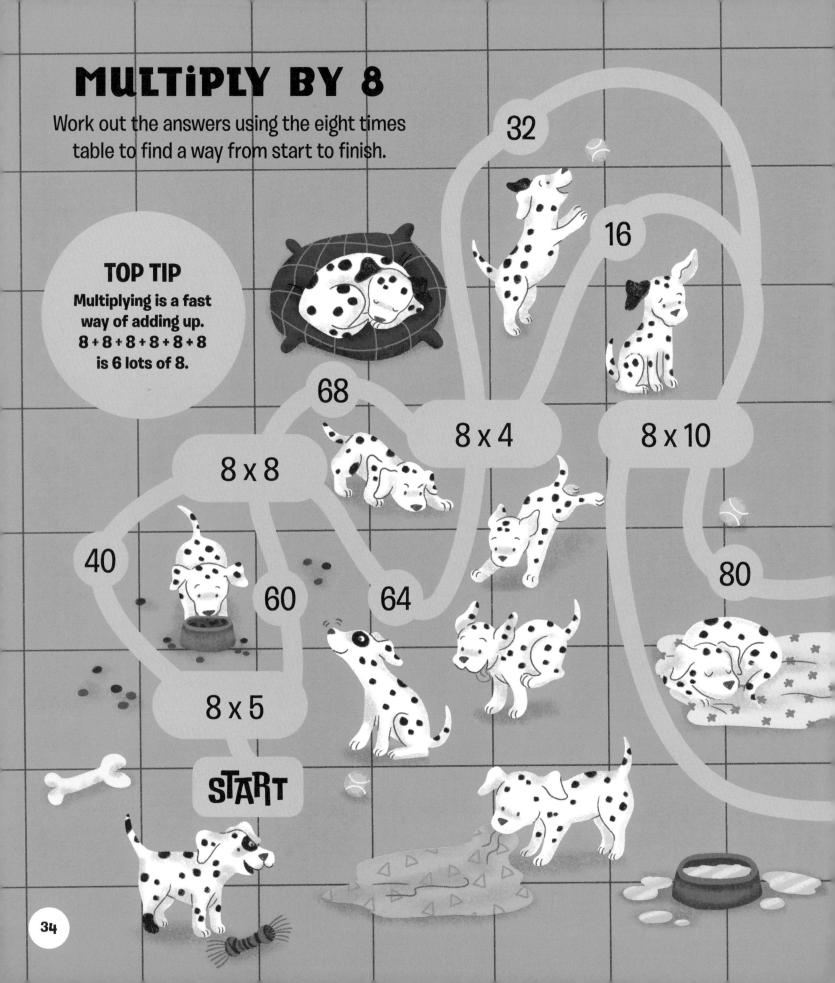

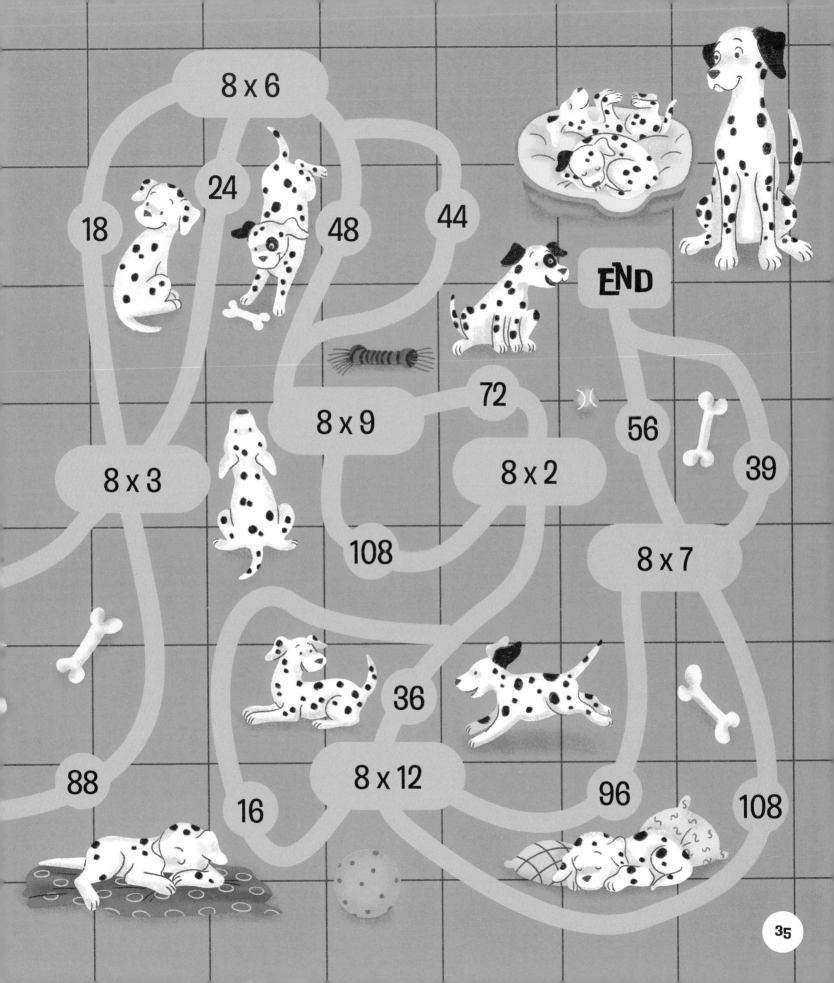

8 x 6

24

18

48

44

END

8 x 9

72

56

39

8 x 3

8 x 2

108

8 x 7

36

88

8 x 12

96

108

16

35

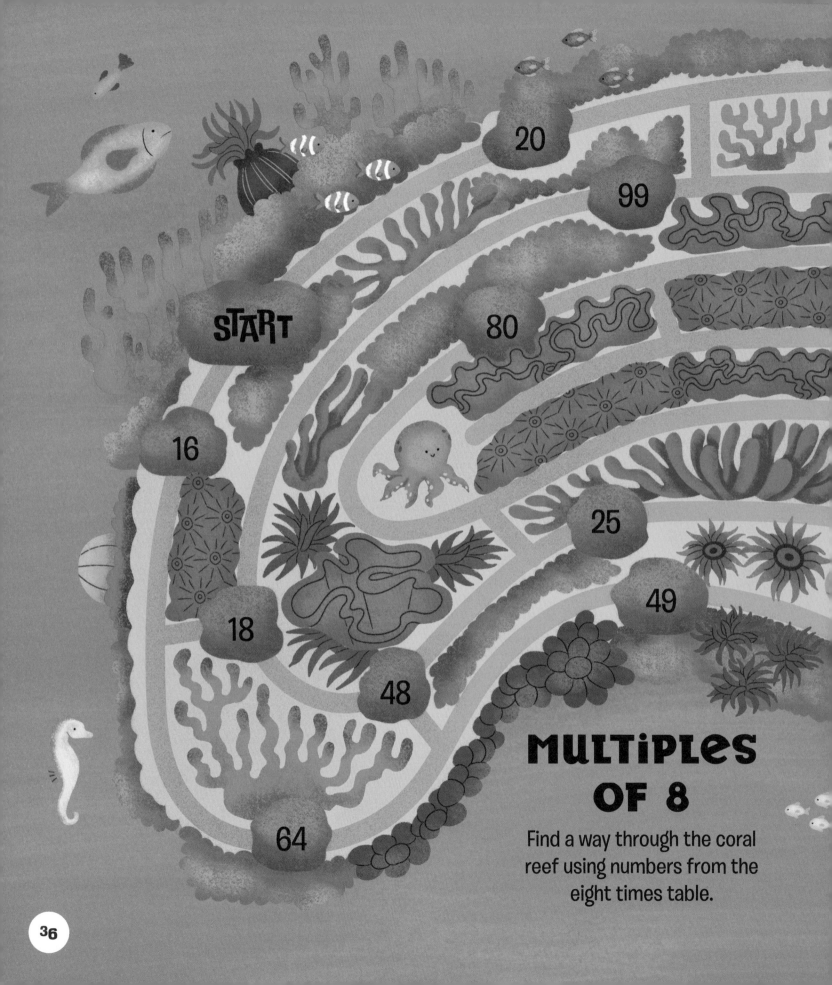

20

99

START

80

16

25

18

49

48

64

MULTIPLES OF 8

Find a way through the coral reef using numbers from the eight times table.

DIVIDING BY 8

Use your eight times table to find a way through this dotty, spotty maze!

4

2

16 ÷ 8

11

9

2

72 ÷ 8

5

END

8 ÷ 8

TOP TIP
Repeating the eight times table over and over will help you to remember it.

0

9

1

48 ÷ 8

6

39

MULTIPLES OF 2, 4, AND 8

Help the farmer with the apple harvest.
Solve the multiplication problems and follow
the correct answers.

12

4 x 7

20

4 x 5

2 x 12

24

21

18

12

26

15

2 x 9

2 x 6

START

TOP TIP

Use the units to help you. All the answers should be even numbers.

28

8 x 3

16

35

4 x 4

24

19

24

64

16

8 x 8

END

4 x 11

24

44

16

8 x 2

42

DIVISION OF 2, 4, AND 8

It's party time! Work out the correct answers to find a route to the piñata.

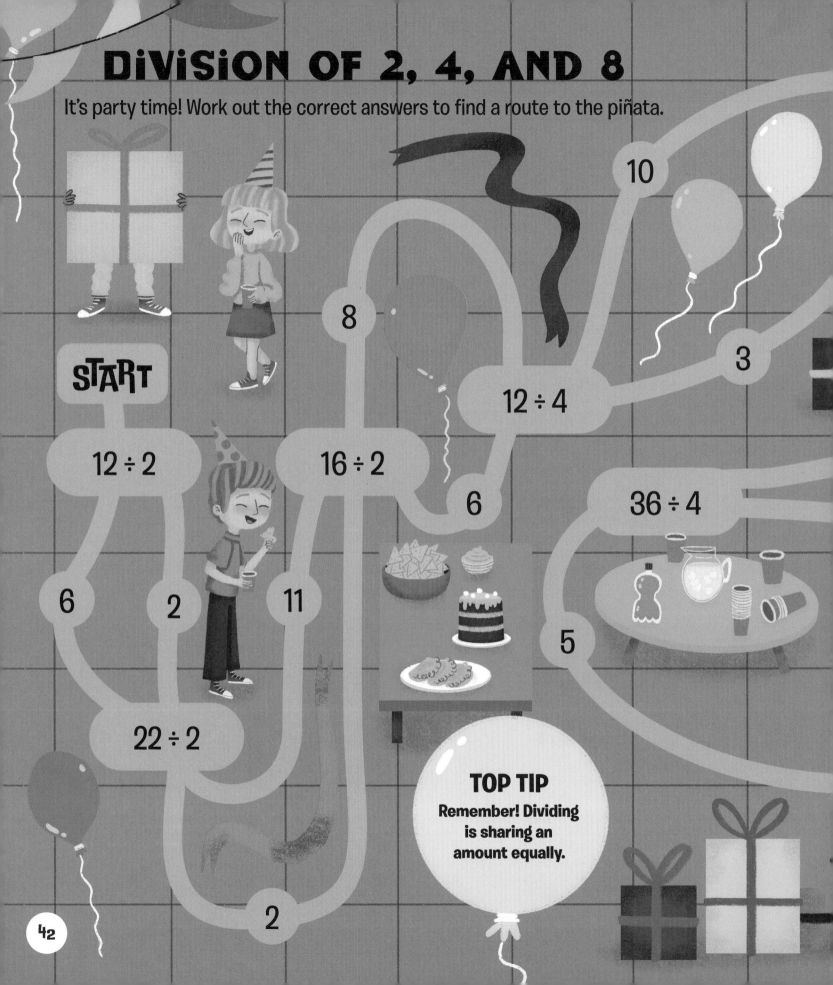

10

3

8

12 ÷ 4

START

12 ÷ 2

16 ÷ 2

6

36 ÷ 4

6

2

11

5

22 ÷ 2

TOP TIP
Remember! Dividing is sharing an amount equally.

2

42

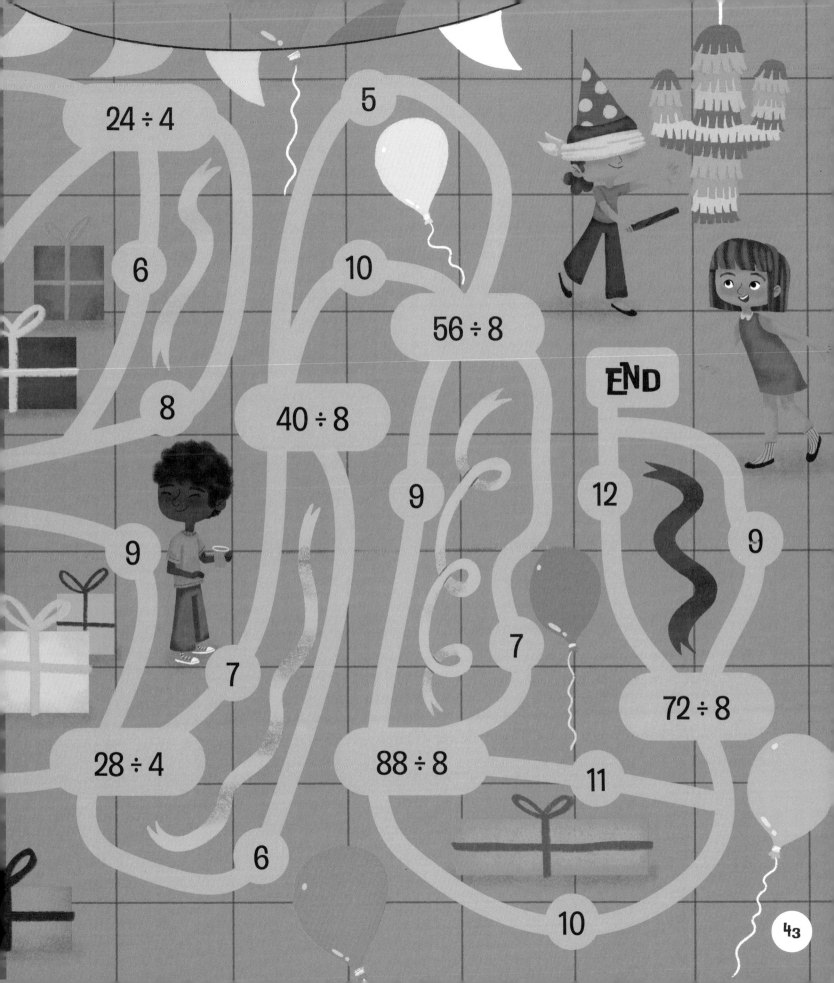

24 ÷ 4

5

10

56 ÷ 8

6

END

8

40 ÷ 8

9

12

9

9

7

7

28 ÷ 4

72 ÷ 8

88 ÷ 8

11

6

10

MULTIPLY BY 3

Find the correct way through this maze full of yummy treats!
The answers are all part of the three times table.

START

3 x 10

0

3

30

3 x 8

3 x 0

24

24

15

20

3 x 5

11

3 x 4

12

8

TOP TIP
Keep counting in threes
to get better at your
three times table.

3 x 9

44

16

6

3 x 7

3 x 6

4

18

3 x 2

21

3 x 3

9

12

18

24

3 x 12

36

13

END

27

3 x 11

33

18

45

START

25   13

24

36

30

27

15

13

18

33

MULTIPLES OF 3

Fly high and find the correct
route using numbers from the
three times table.

46

12

30

TOP TIP

A number is in the three times table if its digits add up to 3, 6, or 9. So 36 is in the three times table because 3 + 6 = 9.

19

16

28

35

6

3

9

21

11

19

END

47

DIVIDING BY 3

Juggle your way across this maze, following a path made by the correct answers.

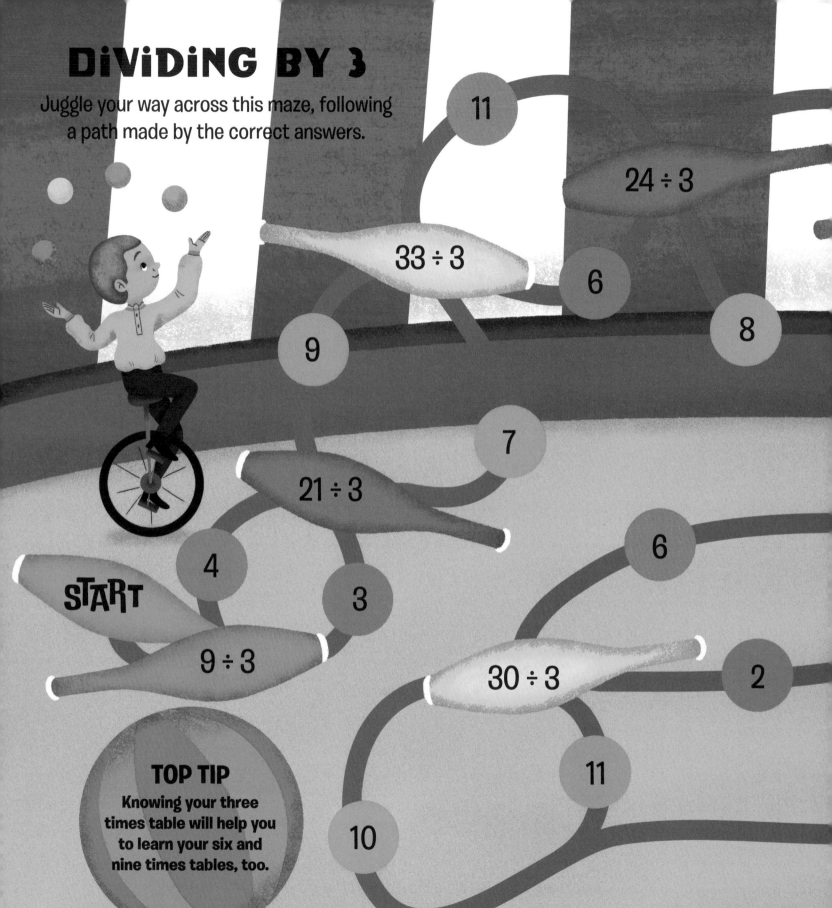

11

24 ÷ 3

33 ÷ 3

6

8

9

7

21 ÷ 3

4

3

6

START

9 ÷ 3

30 ÷ 3

2

11

TOP TIP
Knowing your three times table will help you to learn your six and nine times tables, too.

10

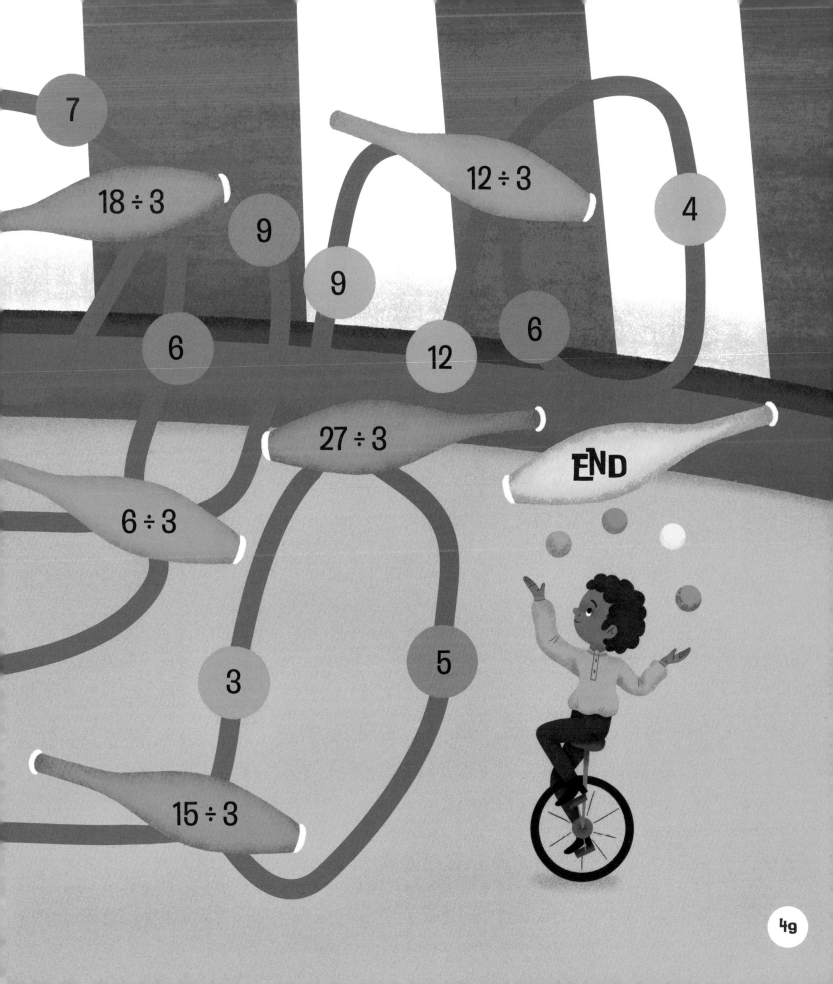

MULTIPLY BY 6

Look out for snowballs as you dash across this wintry scene! Solve each multiplication problem and follow the correct answers.

START

6 x 3

32

12

6 x 7

18

40

6 x 2

42

14

6 x 4

24

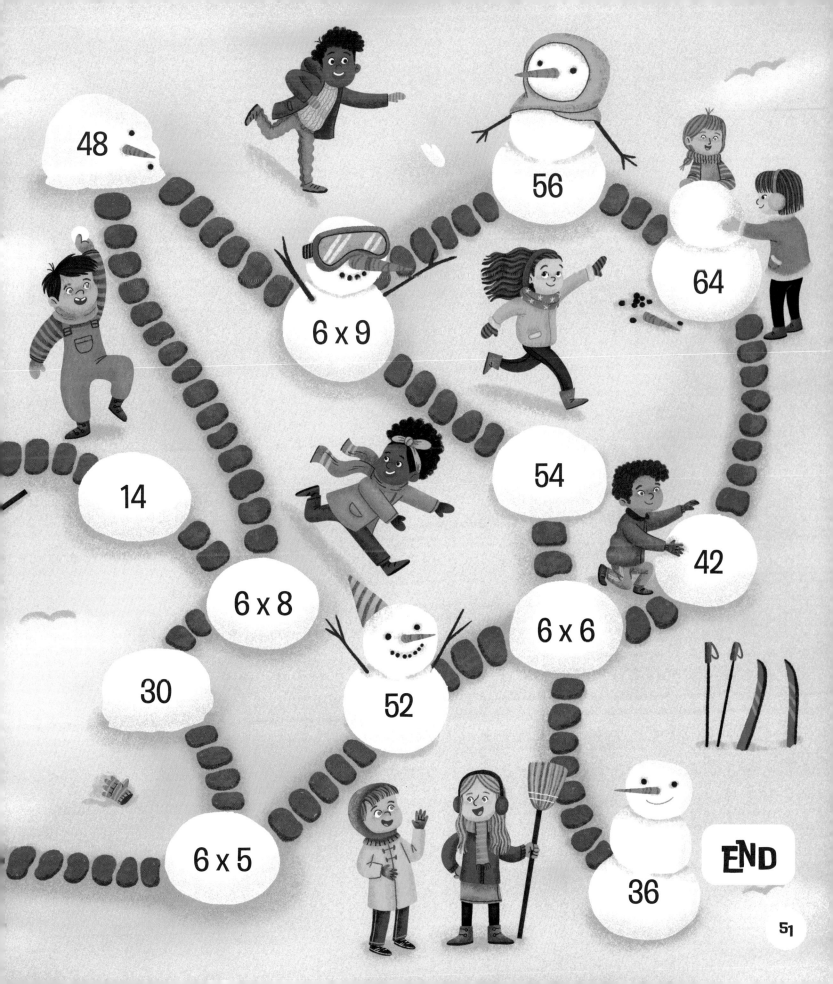

48

56

6 x 9

64

14

54

42

6 x 8

6 x 6

30

52

6 x 5

END

36

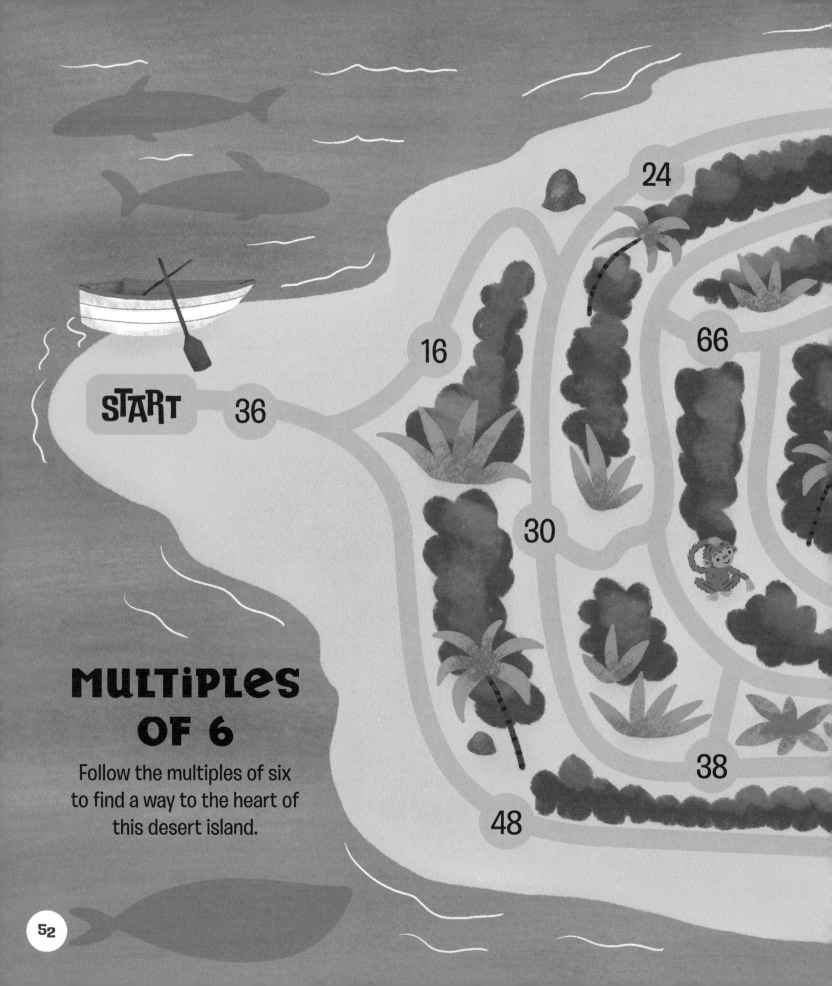

START

36

16

24

66

30

48

38

MULTIPLES OF 6

Follow the multiples of six to find a way to the heart of this desert island.

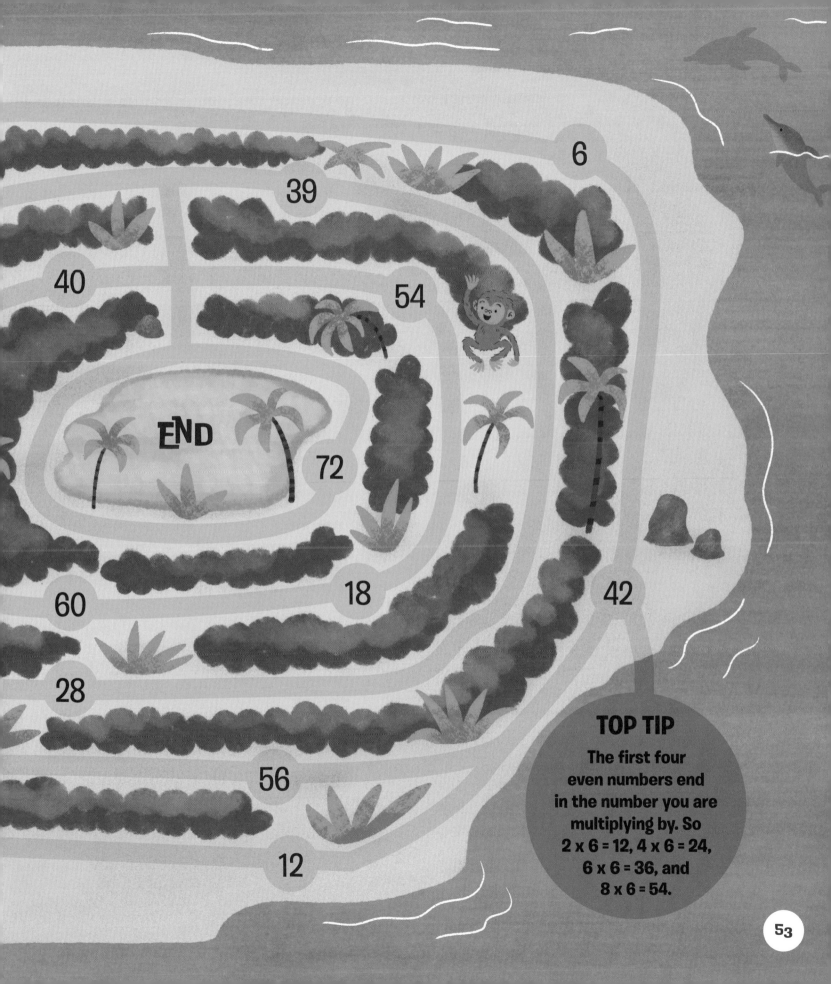

6

39

40

54

72

END

18

60

42

28

56

12

53

TOP TIP

The first four
even numbers end
in the number you are
multiplying by. So
2 x 6 = 12, 4 x 6 = 24,
6 x 6 = 36, and
8 x 6 = 54.

DIVIDING BY 6

Navigate safely past all the slithery snakes.
Follow the path made by the correct answers.

36 ÷ 6

2

9

12 ÷ 6

8

72 ÷ 6

12

8

12

48 ÷ 6

42 ÷ 6

8

7

START

6

12

6

TOP TIP
Stick with it while you
learn the six times table.
It's a little more difficult
than the other even
numbers.

9

$30 \div 6$

12

$54 \div 6$

10

5

6

3

24 ÷ 6

END

4

$18 \div 6$

11

$66 \div 6$

8

MULTIPLY BY 9

Help the skater join his friends by following the multiples of 9.

12

9 x 2

63

9 x 7

56

108

81

9 x 9

54

63

9 x 6

START

TOP TIP

Add up the digits in the solutions for the nine times table and the answer is always 9!

6 x 9 = 54, and 5 + 4 = 9

12 x 9 = 108, and 1 + 0 + 8 = 9

9 x 11

98

72

18

9 x 5

9 x 8

81

99

45

15

36

9 x 4

9 x 12

41

112

108

9 x 10

27

99

END

90

9 x 3

18

MULTIPLES OF 9

Guide the bee back to its home, following numbers from the nine times table.

DIVIDING BY 9

Find the correct answers to help the witch fly through the maze.

8

8

12

54 ÷ 9

TOP TIP

Dividing by 9 is made easier if you round up the tens. For example, 36 rounded up = 40, and 36 ÷ 9 = 4

6

4

72 ÷ 9

18 ÷ 9

2

8

5

7

45 ÷ 9

START

60

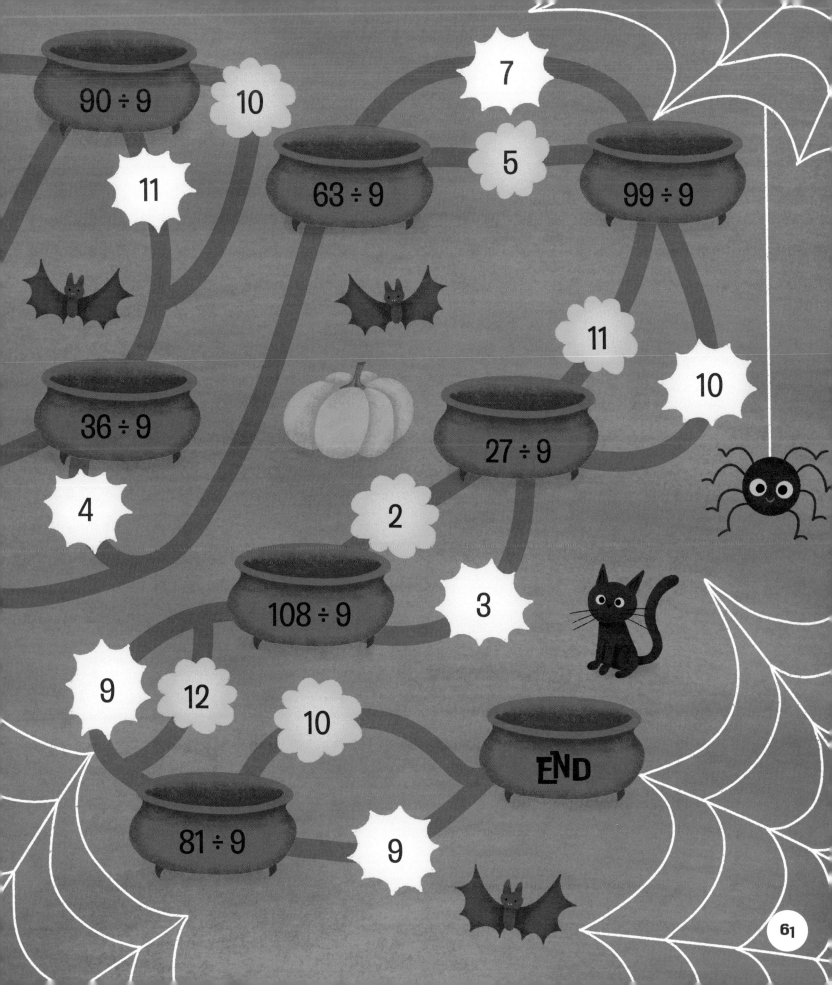

6 x 5

16

36

30

3 x 12

24

3 x 8

34

33

18

15

6 x 7

3 x 6

24

START

42

40

6 x 4

MULTIPLES OF 3, 6, AND 9

Carefully find a way through the maze, working
out the answers to find the route.

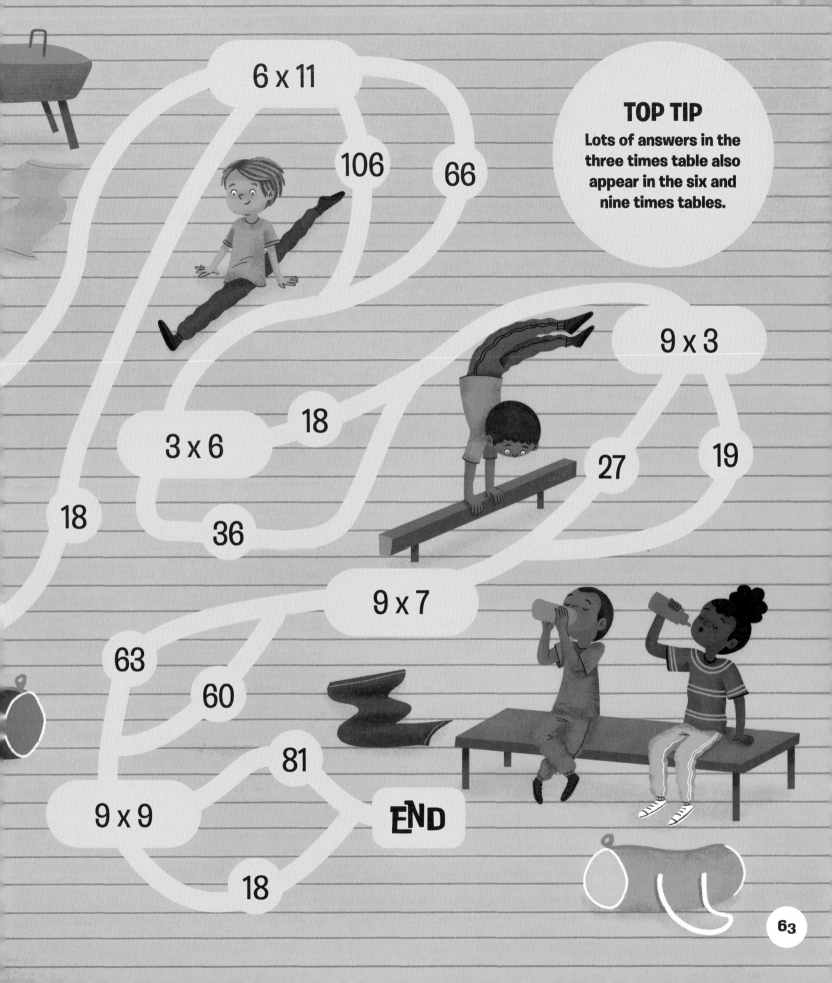

6 x 11

106

66

TOP TIP
Lots of answers in the
three times table also
appear in the six and
nine times tables.

9 x 3

18

3 x 6

27

19

18

36

9 x 7

63

60

81

9 x 9

END

18

63

DIVISION OF 3, 6, AND 9

Bounce between the craters, solving the problems and choosing the correct answer as you go.

6

$18 \div 3$

$63 \div 9$

7

6

7

9

3

$42 \div 6$

10

12

6

$30 \div 3$

$54 \div 9$

START

6

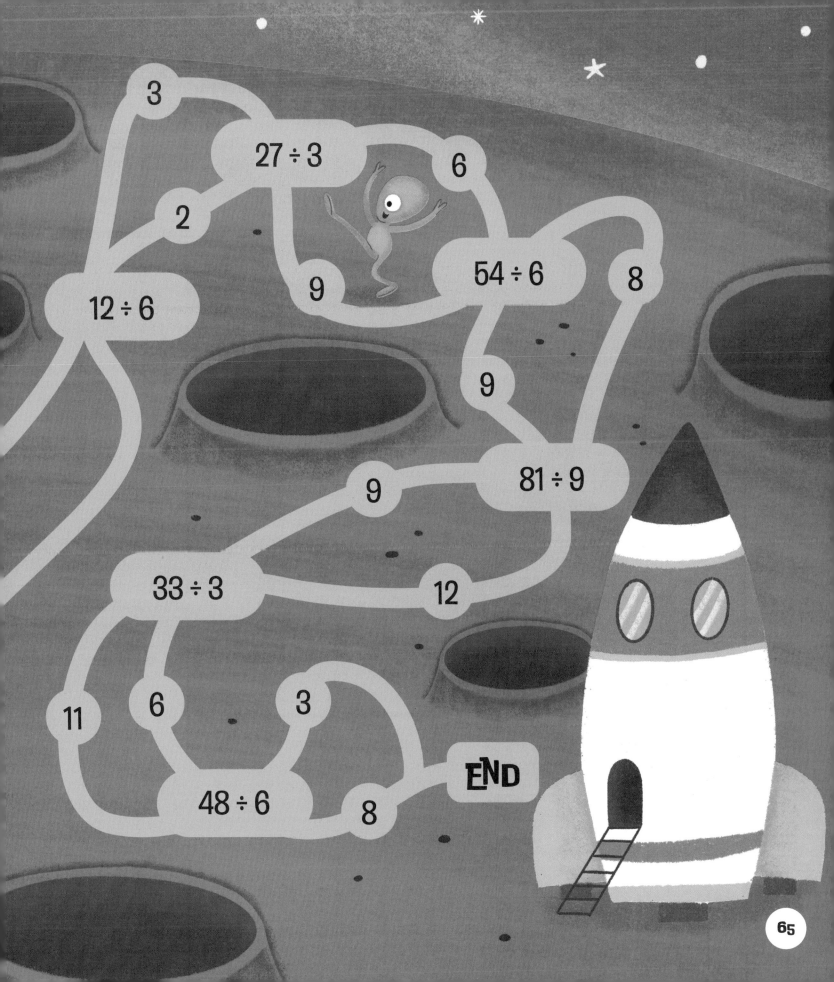

MULTIPLY BY 7

Flutter from flower to flower following a path that uses numbers from the seven times table.

35

7 x 5

32

7 x 4

32

84

START

28

7 x 7

106

49

39

7 x 12

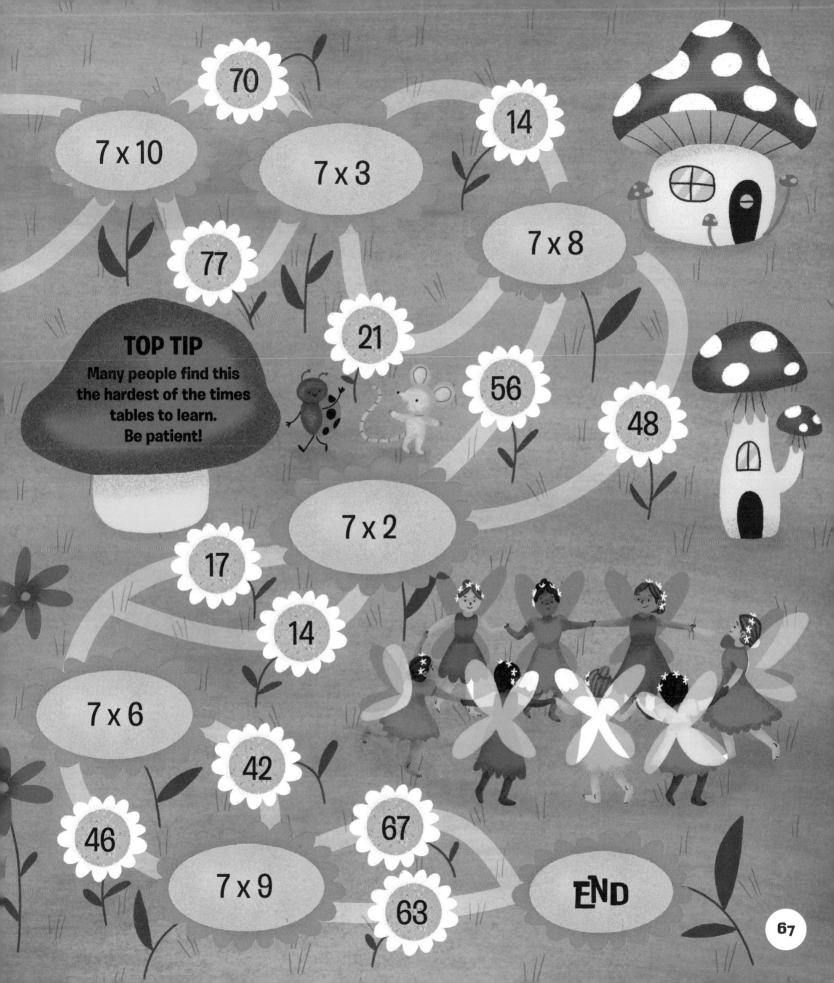

70

7 x 10

7 x 3

14

7 x 8

77

21

TOP TIP
Many people find this
the hardest of the times
tables to learn.
Be patient!

56

48

7 x 2

17

14

7 x 6

42

46

7 x 9

67

63

END

START

MULTIPLES OF 7

Help the tigress get back to her cubs by following numbers from the seven times table.

63
82
28
35
44
45
56
24
60
21

42

81

14

39

70

76

END

49

69

TOP TIP
Remember that you can multiply in any order. Use your knowledge of all the other times tables to help, for example, if you're unsure of 7 x 5, do you know what 5 x 7 is?

DIVIDING BY 7

Ride the waves and follow the route that uses the correct answers to the problems.

TOP TIP

Learning the tricky 7 times table has its uses, because there are 7 days in a week. Once you know it, you can work out that 28 days is 4 weeks, and so on.

9

49 ÷ 7

84 ÷ 7

17

11

7

77 ÷ 7

3

5

14 ÷ 7

8

6

21 ÷ 7

2

START

8

6

56 ÷ 7

8

12

4

8

42 ÷ 7

35 ÷ 7

28 ÷ 7

12

5

7

4

9

70 ÷ 7

63 ÷ 7

10

7

END

MULTIPLY BY 11

Pick your way through the flock of pigeons, using your knowledge of the eleven times table.

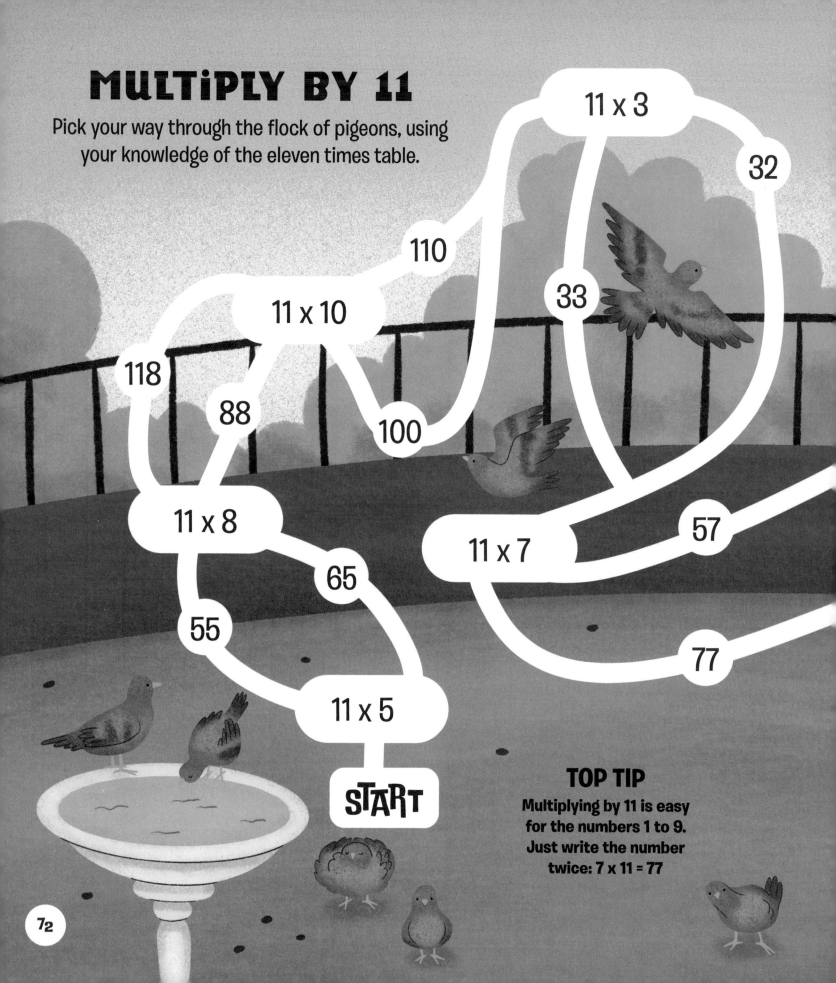

11 x 3

32

110

33

11 x 10

118

88

100

11 x 8

57

65

11 x 7

55

77

11 x 5

START

TOP TIP

Multiplying by 11 is easy for the numbers 1 to 9. Just write the number twice: 7 x 11 = 77

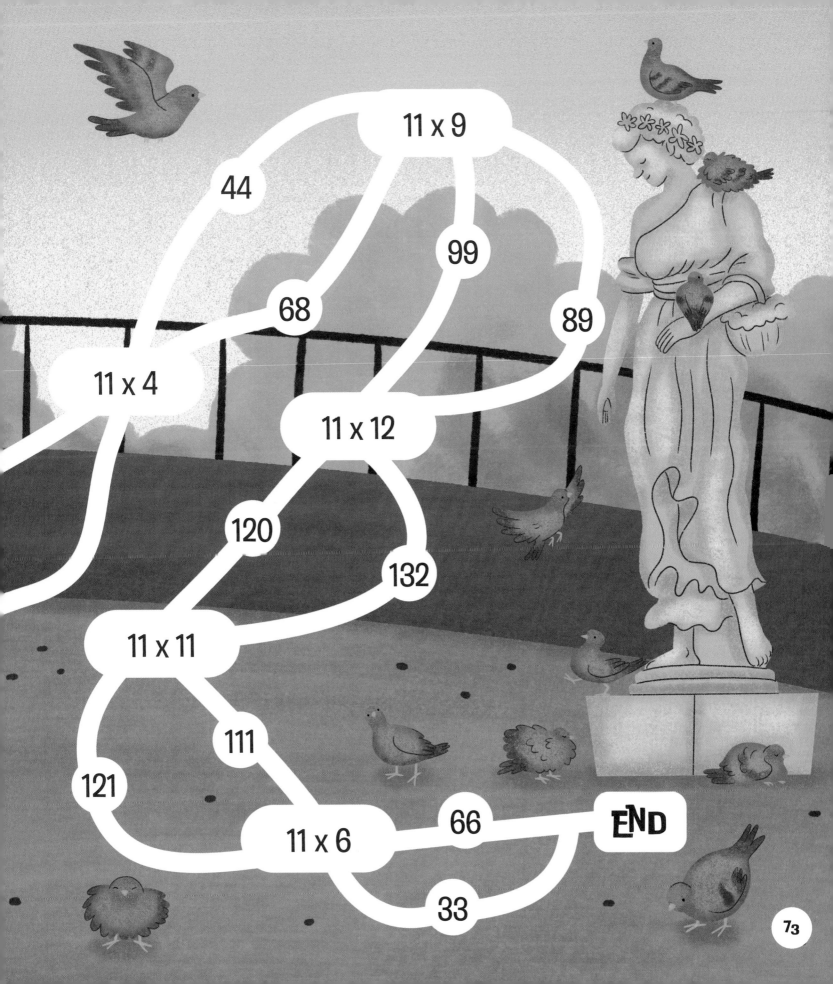

11 x 9

44

99

68

89

11 x 4

11 x 12

120

132

11 x 11

111

121

11 x 6

66

END

33

DIVIDING BY 11

Call at the different parts of the playground, following a path that features all the correct answers.

1

11 ÷ 11

0

5

33 ÷ 11

3

55 ÷ 11

9

8

6

12

13

66 ÷ 11

88 ÷ 11

6

START

74

6

$121 \div 11$

$99 \div 11$ 9

$22 \div 11$ 2

11

12

10

5

12

$132 \div 11$

$77 \div 11$

$44 \div 11$ 8

7   10

4

TOP TIP

Dividing by 11 is straightforward—the answer is there twice, for the numbers up to 9!

END

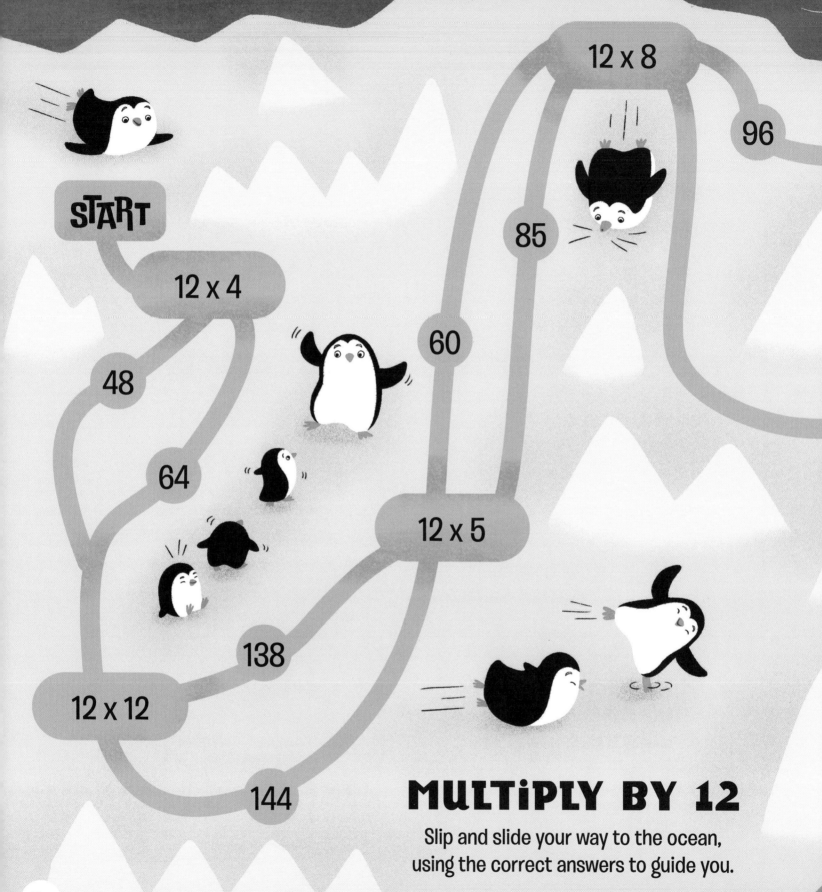

START

12 x 4

48

64

12 x 12

138

144

12 x 8

96

85

60

12 x 5

MULTIPLY BY 12

Slip and slide your way to the ocean, using the correct answers to guide you.

76

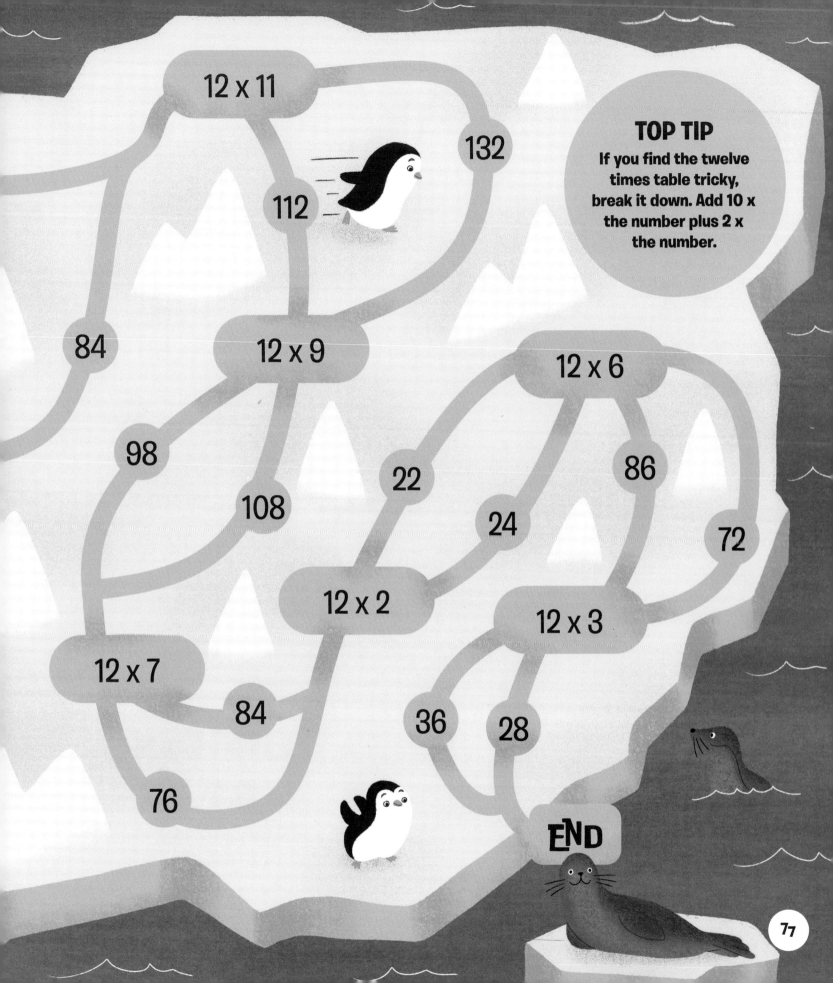

12 x 11

132

112

TOP TIP
If you find the twelve times table tricky, break it down. Add 10 x the number plus 2 x the number.

84

12 x 9

12 x 6

98

22

86

108

24

72

12 x 2

12 x 3

12 x 7

84

36

28

76

END

77

9

12

$144 \div 12$

$60 \div 12$

START

2

5

$48 \div 12$

12

4

8

$24 \div 12$

7

$72 \div 12$

DIVIDING BY 12

Fly through the skies, following a route made by the correct answers.

6

6

$96 \div 12$

3

8

$36 \div 12$

7

12

12

$120 \div 12$

10

$84 \div 12$

4

$132 \div 12$

7

9

11

END

Multiples of 10, 11, and 12

Navigate a way across the waves to get to the island. Your route should follow multiples of 10, 11, or 12.

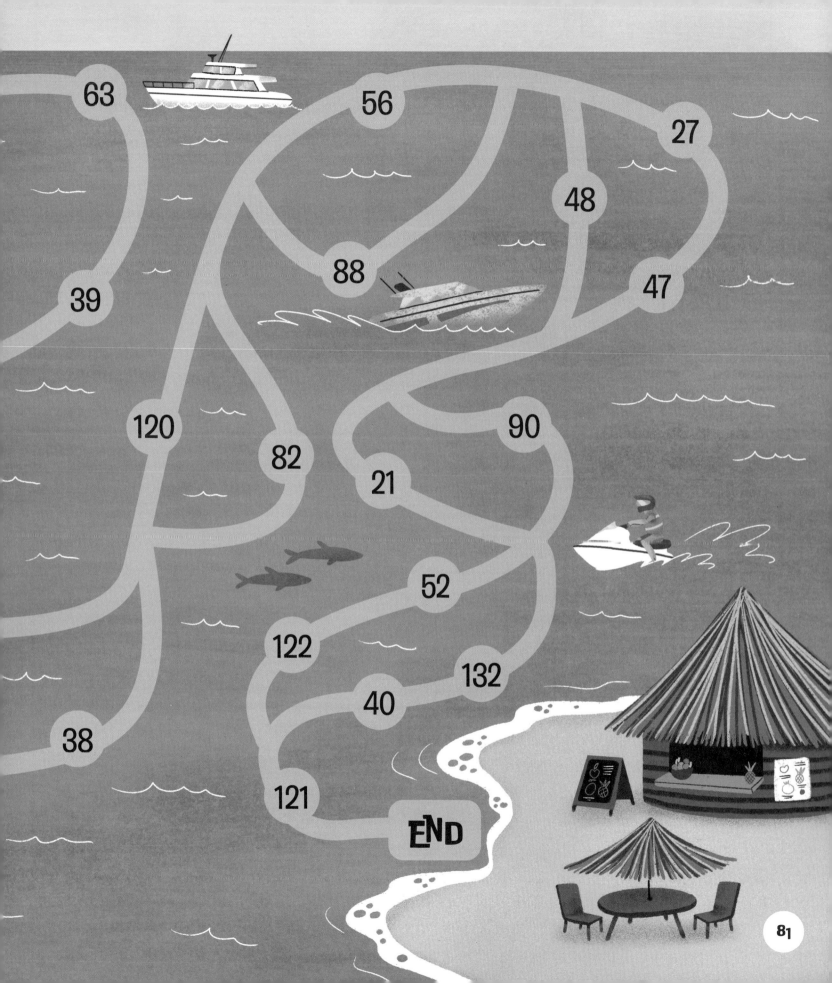

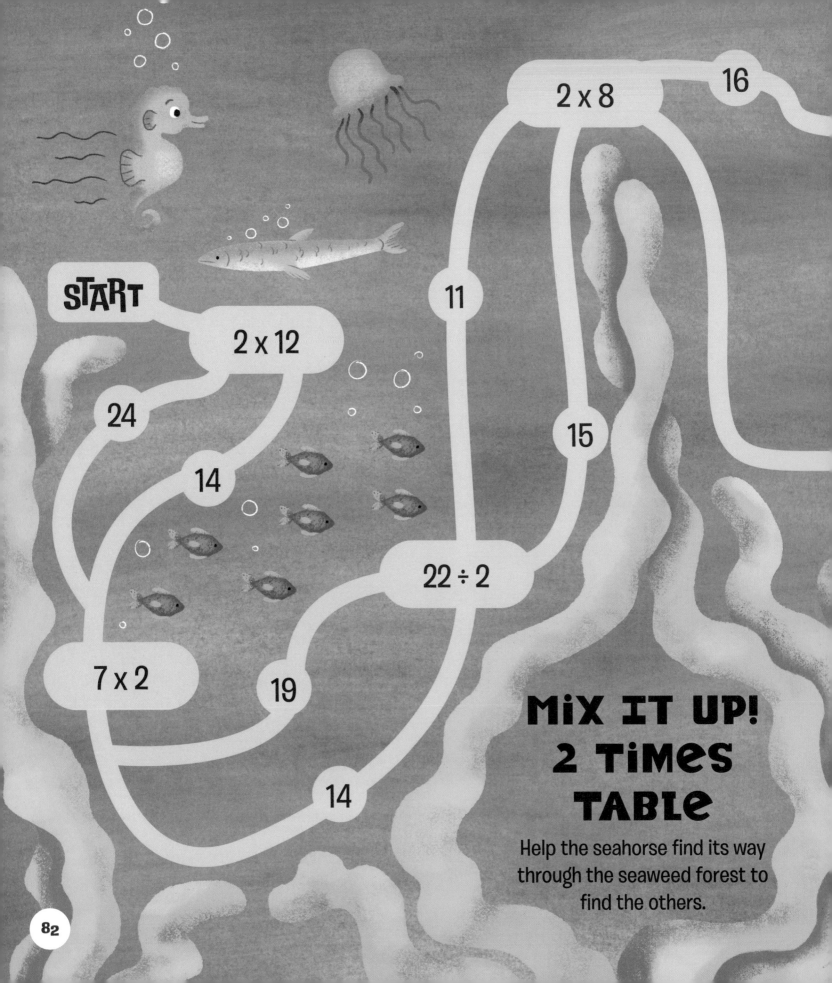

START

2 x 12

24

14

7 x 2

19

14

2 x 8

16

11

15

22 ÷ 2

MiX IT UP!
2 TiMES
TABLE

Help the seahorse find its way
through the seaweed forest to
find the others.

82

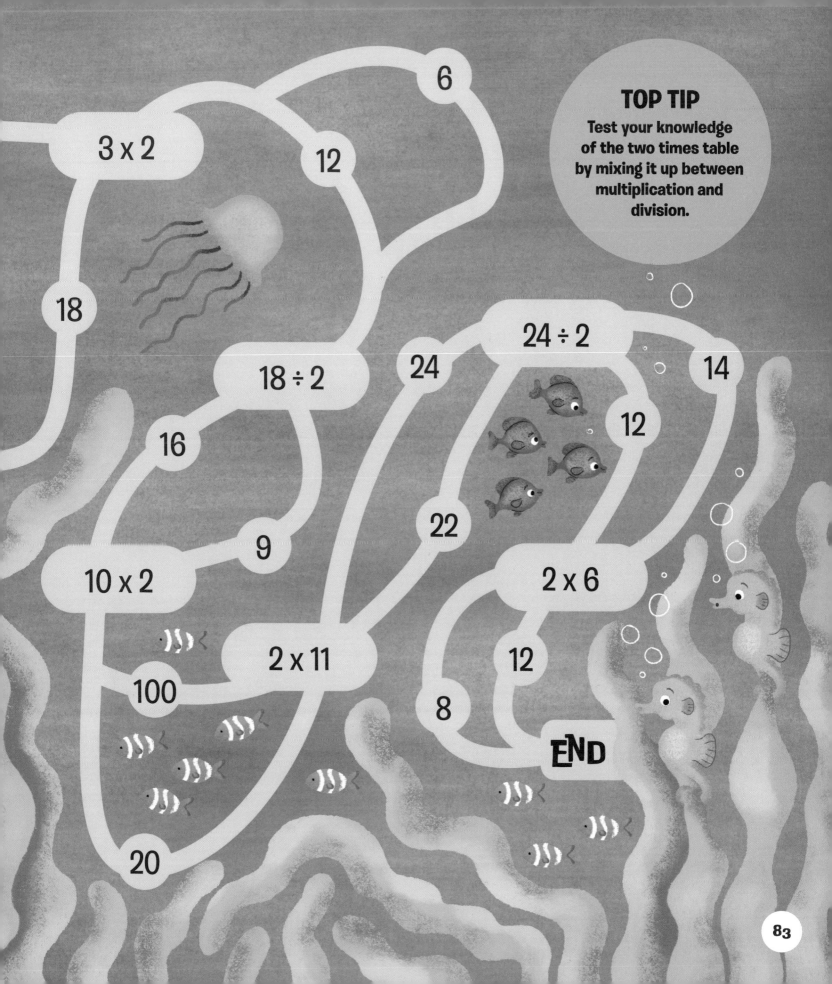

6

3 x 2

12

TOP TIP
Test your knowledge
of the two times table
by mixing it up between
multiplication and
division.

18

24 ÷ 2

24

14

18 ÷ 2

12

16

22

9

10 x 2

2 x 6

2 x 11

12

100

8

END

20

84

5 TIMES TABLE

How many cookies do you gather if you follow the correct answers along the path in Candy Forest?

20

5 x 12

80

60

125

45 ÷ 5

5

15

12 x 5

40

60

25 ÷ 5

6

END

60 ÷ 5

12

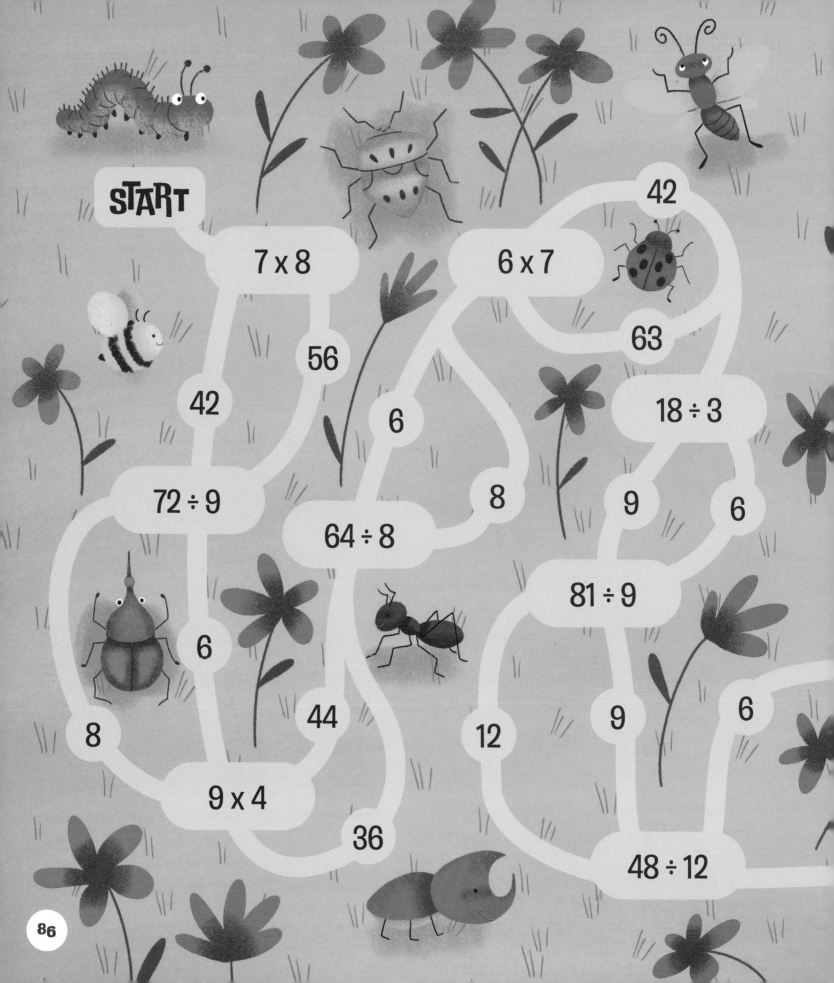

START

7 x 8

6 x 7

42

56

63

42

18 ÷ 3

72 ÷ 9

6

8

9

6

64 ÷ 8

81 ÷ 9

6

44

12

9

6

8

9 x 4

36

48 ÷ 12

MiX iT UP! THE TRiCKY ONE!

Work your way from start to finish, finding the correct answers to some of the more difficult problems from the times tables.

TOP TIP

Take it slowly and don't rush. It can be hard to jump from one times table to another.

63

6 x 8

69

56

9 x 7

48

36

48

END

6 x 6

4

MULTIPLES OF 25

Follow the snail trail to find some juicy treats at the end!

25

195

START

125

65

150

175

45

75

135

50

100

END

185

55

TOP TIP
Think of 25s as four
quarters of 100.

ANSWERS

PAGES 4–5

3 + 3 = 6	4 + 4 = 8	10 + 10 = 20
6 + 6 = 12	8 + 8 = 16	7 + 7 = 14

PAGES 6–7

2 x 5 = 10	2 x 10 = 20	2 x 4 = 8
2 x 7 = 14	2 x 9 = 18	2 x 8 = 16

PAGES 8–9

4	18	16
20	6	14
12	2	
8	10	

PAGES 10–11

16 ÷ 2 = 8	22 ÷ 2 = 11	14 ÷ 2 = 7
12 ÷ 2 = 6	10 ÷ 2 = 5	6 ÷ 2 = 3
24 ÷ 2 = 12	18 ÷ 2 = 9	20 ÷ 2 = 10

PAGES 12-13

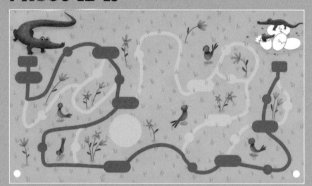

10 x 4 = 40   10 x 10 = 100   10 x 3 = 30
10 x 7 = 70   10 x 8 = 80   10 x 6 = 60

PAGES 14-15

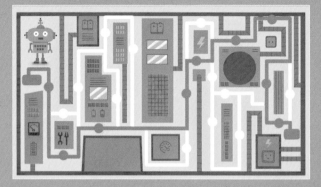

20   60   40
50   10   70
90   80   100

PAGES 16-17

70 ÷ 10 = 7   50 ÷ 10 = 5   60 ÷ 10 = 6
90 ÷ 10 = 9   120 ÷ 10 = 12   10 ÷ 10 = 1
40 ÷ 10 = 4   30 ÷ 10 = 3   100 ÷ 10 = 10
20 ÷ 10 = 2   80 ÷ 10 = 8
90 ÷ 10 = 9   110 ÷ 10 = 11

PAGES 18-19

5 x 10 = 50   5 x 2 = 10   5 x 6 = 30
5 x 7 = 35   5 x 4 = 20   5 x 12 = 60
5 x 3 = 15   5 x 11 = 55
5 x 5 = 25   5 x 8 = 40

PAGES 20-21

15   20   10
35   45   40
60   55   25

PAGES 22-23

25 ÷ 5 = 5   35 ÷ 5 = 7   55 ÷ 5 = 11
50 ÷ 5 = 10   45 ÷ 5 = 9   60 ÷ 5 = 12
30 ÷ 5 = 6   40 ÷ 5 = 8
15 ÷ 5 = 3   10 ÷ 5 = 2

PAGES 24-25

2 x 6 = 12   10 x 3 = 30   5 x 3 = 15
2 x 12 - 24   10 x 5 = 50   5 x 8 = 40
2 x 9 = 18   10 x 10 = 100   5 x 11 = 55
10 x 8 = 80   5 x 5 = 25

PAGES 26-27

80 ÷ 10 = 8   45 ÷ 5 = 9   22 ÷ 2 = 11
30 ÷ 10 = 3   20 ÷ 5 = 4   18 ÷ 2 = 9
100 ÷ 10 = 10   15 ÷ 5 = 3
60 ÷ 10 = 6   35 ÷ 5 = 7

PAGES 28-29

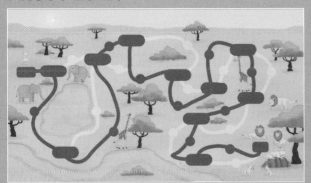

4 x 2 = 8   4 x 8 = 32   4 x 4 = 16
4 x 7 = 28   4 x 3 = 12   4 x 9 = 36
4 x 5 = 20   4 x 6 = 24
4 x 11 = 44   4 x 10 = 40

PAGES 30-31

40   32   28
8   44   16
20   4   36
12   24
48   12

PAGES 32-33

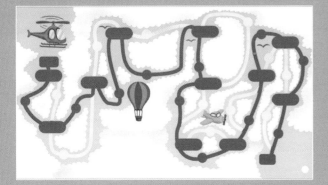

16 ÷ 4 = 4   44 ÷ 4 = 11   36 ÷ 4 = 9
24 ÷ 4 = 6   32 ÷ 4 = 8   20 ÷ 4 = 5
12 ÷ 4 = 3   28 ÷ 4 = 7   8 ÷ 4 = 2
48 ÷ 4 = 12   40 ÷ 4 = 10

PAGES 34-35

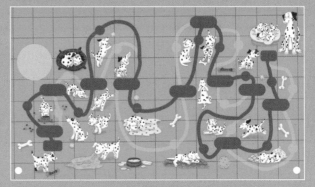

8 x 5 = 40   8 x 3 = 24   8 x 12 = 96
8 x 8 = 64   8 x 6 = 48   8 x 7 = 56
8 x 4 = 32   8 x 9 = 72
8 x 10 = 80   8 x 2 = 16

PAGES 36-37

16	24	40
64	56	72
48	80	
80	32	

PAGES 38-39

$80 \div 8 = 10$	$88 \div 8 = 11$	$8 \div 8 = 1$
$24 \div 8 = 3$	$32 \div 8 = 4$	$48 \div 8 = 6$
$40 \div 8 = 5$	$72 \div 8 = 9$	
$56 \div 8 = 7$	$16 \div 8 = 2$	

PAGES 40-41

$2 \times 6 = 12$	$4 \times 7 = 28$	$8 \times 8 = 64$
$2 \times 9 = 18$	$4 \times 4 = 16$	$8 \times 3 = 24$
$2 \times 12 = 24$	$4 \times 11 = 44$	
$4 \times 5 = 20$	$8 \times 2 = 16$	

PAGES 42-43

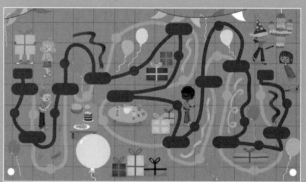

$12 \div 2 = 6$	$24 \div 4 = 6$	$56 \div 8 = 7$
$22 \div 2 = 11$	$36 \div 4 = 9$	$88 \div 8 = 11$
$16 \div 2 = 8$	$28 \div 4 = 7$	$72 \div 8 = 9$
$12 \div 4 = 3$	$40 \div 8 = 5$	

PAGES 44-45

$3 \times 8 = 24$	$3 \times 6 = 18$	$3 \times 12 = 36$
$3 \times 5 = 15$	$3 \times 2 = 6$	$3 \times 4 = 12$
$3 \times 0 = 0$	$3 \times 7 = 21$	$3 \times 9 = 27$
$3 \times 10 = 30$	$3 \times 3 = 9$	$3 \times 11 = 33$

PAGES 46-47

27	24	3
15	36	21
33	6	9
18	12	
30	30	

PAGES 48-49

9 ÷ 3 = 3	18 ÷ 3 = 6	27 ÷ 3 = 9
21 ÷ 3 = 7	6 ÷ 3 = 2	12 ÷ 3 = 4
33 ÷ 3 = 11	30 ÷ 3 = 10	
24 ÷ 3 = 8	15 ÷ 3 = 5	

PAGES 50-51

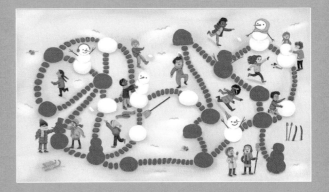

6 x 3 = 18	6 x 5 = 30	6 x 9 = 54
6 x 7 = 42	6 x 8 = 48	6 x 6 = 36
6 x 4 = 24		

PAGES 52-53

36	6	60
48	24	18
12	30	54
42	66	72

PAGES 54-55

48 ÷ 6 = 8	24 ÷ 6 = 4	54 ÷ 6 = 9
12 ÷ 6 = 2	42 ÷ 6 = 7	30 ÷ 6 = 5
72 ÷ 6 = 12	66 ÷ 6 = 11	
36 ÷ 6 = 6	18 ÷ 6 = 3	

PAGES 56-57

9 x 6 = 54	9 x 11 = 99	9 x 12 = 108
9 x 9 = 81	9 x 8 = 72	9 x 10 = 90
9 x 7 = 63	9 x 5 = 45	9 x 3 = 27
9 x 2 = 18	9 x 4 = 36	

PAGES 58-59

18	72	81
63	27	9
90	45	99
54	36	108

PAGES 60–61

45 ÷ 9 = 5	90 ÷ 9 = 10	27 ÷ 9 = 3
72 ÷ 9 = 8	36 ÷ 9 = 4	108 ÷ 9 = 12
54 ÷ 9 = 6	63 ÷ 9 = 7	81 ÷ 9 = 9
18 ÷ 9 = 2	99 ÷ 9 = 11	

PAGES 62–63

3 x 6 = 18	6 x 7 = 42	9 x 3 = 27
3 x 12 = 36	6 x 4 = 24	9 x 7 = 63
3 x 8 = 24	6 x 11 = 66	9 x 9 = 81
6 x 5 = 30	3 x 6 = 18	

PAGES 64–65

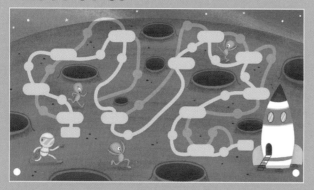

30 ÷ 3 = 10	54 ÷ 9 = 6	81 ÷ 9 = 9
42 ÷ 6 = 7	12 ÷ 6 = 2	33 ÷ 3 = 11
63 ÷ 9 = 7	27 ÷ 3 = 9	48 ÷ 6 = 8
18 ÷ 3 = 6	54 ÷ 6 = 9	

PAGES 66–67

7 x 4 = 28	7 x 10 = 70	7 x 6 = 42
7 x 7 = 49	7 x 3 = 21	7 x 9 = 63
7 x 12 = 84	7 x 8 = 56	
7 x 5 = 35	7 x 2 = 14	

PAGES 68–69

35	14	21
28	70	49
42	56	

PAGES 70–71

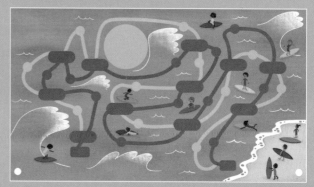

21 ÷ 7 = 3	56 ÷ 7 = 8	42 ÷ 7 = 6
77 ÷ 7 = 11	28 ÷ 7 = 4	35 ÷ 7 = 5
49 ÷ 7 = 7	14 ÷ 7 = 2	70 ÷ 7 = 10
84 ÷ 7 = 12	63 ÷ 7 = 9	

Pages 72-73

11 x 5 = 55	11 x 7 = 77	11 x 11 = 121
11 x 8 = 88	11 x 4 = 44	11 x 6 = 66
11 x 10 = 110	11 x 9 = 99	
11 x 3 = 33	11 x 12 = 132	

Pages 74-75

88 ÷ 11 = 8	11 ÷ 11 = 1	99 ÷ 11 = 9
33 ÷ 11 = 3	121 ÷ 11 = 11	22 ÷ 11 = 2
55 ÷ 11 = 5	44 ÷ 11 = 4	77 ÷ 11 = 7
66 ÷ 11 = 6	132 ÷ 11 = 12	

Pages 76-77

12 x 4 = 48	12 x 11 = 132	12 x 6 = 72
12 x 12 = 144	12 x 9 = 108	12 x 3 = 36
12 x 5 = 60	12 x 7 = 84	
12 x 8 = 96	12 x 2 = 24	

Pages 78-79

48 ÷ 12 = 4	60 ÷ 12 = 5	132 ÷ 12 = 11
72 ÷ 12 = 6	36 ÷ 12 = 3	84 ÷ 12 = 7
24 ÷ 12 = 2	96 ÷ 12 = 8	
144 ÷ 12 = 12	120 ÷ 12 = 10	

Pages 80-81

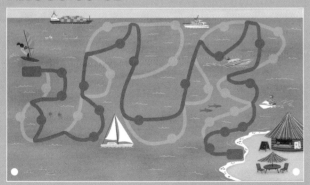

80	55	36	90
66	72	120	132
96	84	88	40
50	30	48	121

Pages 82-83

2 x 12 = 24	3 x 2 = 6	24 ÷ 2 = 12
7 x 2 = 14	18 ÷ 2 = 9	2 x 6 = 12
22 ÷ 2 = 11	10 x 2 = 20	
2 x 8 = 16	2 x 11 = 22	

PAGES 84–85

5 x 7 = 35
4 x 5 = 20
5 x 12 = 60
45 ÷ 5 = 9
12 cookies

10 x 5 = 50
5 x 3 = 15
8 x 5 = 40
5 x 11 = 55

9 x 5 = 45
60 ÷ 5 = 12
25 ÷ 5 = 5
12 x 5 = 60

PAGES 86–87

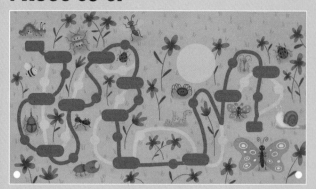

7 x 8 = 56
72 ÷ 9 = 8
9 x 4 = 36
64 ÷ 8 = 8

6 x 7 = 42
18 ÷ 3 = 6
81 ÷ 9 = 9
48 ÷ 12 = 4

6 x 6 = 36
9 x 7 = 63
6 x 8 = 48

PAGES 88

125   25   100
75   175
160   50

TIMES TABLE SQUARE

1	2	3	4	5	6	7	8	9	10	11	12
2	4	6	8	10	12	14	16	18	20	22	24
3	6	9	12	15	18	21	24	28	30	33	36
4	8	12	16	20	24	28	32	36	40	44	48
5	10	15	20	25	30	35	40	45	50	55	60
6	12	18	24	30	36	42	48	54	60	66	72
7	14	21	28	35	42	49	56	63	70	77	84
8	16	24	32	40	48	56	64	72	80	88	96
9	18	27	36	45	54	63	72	81	90	99	108
10	20	30	40	50	60	70	80	90	100	110	120
11	22	33	44	55	66	77	88	99	110	121	132
12	24	36	48	60	72	84	96	108	120	132	144